SIMPLE ANSWERS:
Life Is More Than
Just About Money

BY
NICOLE N. MIDDENDORF, CDFA

IGI Press · Minneapolis

IGI Press
241 First Avenue North
Minneapolis, MN 55401 U.S.A.

Website address: www.igipublishing.com

Library of Congress Cataloging-in-Publication Data

Middendorf, Nicole N.
    Life is more than just about money : simple answers / by Nicole N. Middendorf.
       p. cm.
    ISBN 978-0-9799963-1-3
    1. Finance, Personal. 2. Investments. 3. Retirement income—Planning. 4. New business enterprises—Management. I. Title.
    HG179.M4568 2008
    332.024—dc2   2008009114

Manufactured in the United States of America
1 2 3 4 5 6 - BP - 13 12 11 10 09 08

CONTENTS

ACKNOWLEDGEMENTS

I want to extend a thank you to those around me that have made me who I am and have been there to keep me on track.

I owe a big thank-you to my family for supporting my workaholic attitude and keeping me going. To Brad, my husband and No. 1 cheerleader, thank you for being there in the good times and the bad. Thank you to Les and Kay, the couple who always had time to listen to our outlandish ideas, and help us think about all the endless possibilities in life. To my aunt Jane, thank you for all your never-ending support and guidance. You are a true inspiration.

Thank you to Billy, a great supporter, educator, and friend, for your wisdom and your experience. You are truly an invaluable friend.

Thank you to my clients. I love working with you and helping you achieve your dreams. You motivate me and keep me working to give 110 percent.

Thank you to Judy, my editor, for working with me to help fulfill my dreams of publishing a book to help people feel comfortable with and in control of their money.

To the one man who is unstoppable, Dr. George Farrah, thank you for making a difference in my life and the lives of those around you. To fellow business owners, thank you for your stories, ideas, and experiences. Thank you for being a motivation and a source of ideas. And always remember, life is more than just about money.

Nicole N. Middendorf, CDFA
LPL Financial Advisor
President
Strategic Financial, Inc.
www.helpingyouinvest.com

ABOUT THE AUTHOR

Nicole N. Middendorf is a registered representative with LPL Financial and founder of Strategic Financial, Inc. in Plymouth, Minnesota. In 2003, after working as a financial advisor with an investment firm, she struck out on her own as an independent financial advisor. The same year, she was named one of the 25 Women to Watch by *The Business Journal*, was the recipient of the National Association of Women Business Owners (NAWBO) "Woman on the Way" award, and was honored with the Woman of Achievement Award from the TwinWest Chamber of Commerce in Minnesota. She also began as the weekly radio talk-show host for "More Than Money" on WFMP in Minneapolis. Since then, she has been the recipient of numerous awards: a finalist for the Emerging Entrepreneur of the Year award from the TwinWest Chamber of Commerce in 2005, the Minnesota NAWBO Young Business Woman of the Year in 2006, and the Top Women in Finance award from *Finance and Commerce* newspaper in 2007. She appears frequently on numerous local and national television shows discussing various topics about money.

Nicole has undergone extensive professional training in retirement planning for small businesses and practical investments for the general public. She is active in her community and with her clients to empower women and men about money and achieving their financial goals and dreams. To that end, she founded Strategic Financial to help other financial advisors go independent and to help individuals work to achieve financial independence. You can learn more about Nicole and Strategic Financial at www.helpingyouinvest.com.

Congratulations for taking a big step: picking up a book about money. You are about to begin a journey that I hope will help you grow financially. My goal is to inspire you to take control of your money and enable you to inspire those around you in the same way.

Each chapter in this book begins with a brief introduction, followed by a question-and-answer format so you can zero in on the issues and questions that apply to your life right now.

To learn, you don't have to know the "right" questions, you just need to ask the questions that come to your mind. You *do* need to be in the right frame of mind and have the desire to learn, be willing to accept what you don't know, and realize that we all learn the most through living and doing. That means, of course, that we learn by making mistakes. But that can take time; my goal is that the questions and answers in this book will help reduce your mistakes and streamline your path to financial independence.

If you had asked me 15 years ago, I never thought I would read a book about money, let alone write one about it. For me, money was simply a vehicle for getting the things I wanted. Then I married a financial advisor. I made the same excuses many women make: that my husband would take care of the money – which he did. But I realized none of us should ever leave our finances to someone else. We need to learn the answers to our questions so we can achieve financial independence.

I first became excited about money and understood its value when my husband came home one day and told me I should be saving another $100 a month. I thought he was crazy – I was contributing to my 401(k) and my IRA, and he wanted me to save even more for the future? I told him the only way I would save the money is if it were to go for a trip to Australia in three years. So I started investing $100 a month for almost a year.

Pretty soon I noticed that the account totaled more than $3,000. What made the money real wasn't that the account was growing (though I'm sure that helped!). What made it real was that I had attached a goal – saving $100 a month – to a dream – going to Australia. Now, as a financial advisor, my mission is that no one will say what I said: "Someone else takes care of my money."

I always get asked if we went to Australia. We haven't – yet. When I started Strategic Financial we used the money I'd put away to help start the business. We still have our Australian dream, but there's no question the money went to an equally fulfilling dream.

This book, then, comes from my years as a financial advisor fielding questions from seminars, my radio show, television, magazines, and clients. My goal is to get you excited about – not scared of – money. As you read through the questions in this book, my hope is that you see that money in itself is not that complicated; it is we, as individuals, who make it complicated. And as I share these questions with you that you will see there is never a dumb question when it comes to money.

CHAPTER 1

MONEY COMING AND GOING

Money is simply a vehicle. It is your choice. Every morning when you wake up, you have the choice to be in a good mood or a bad mood. When it comes to your money you also have a choice. Every time you choose to spend money, you are, by default, choosing not to spend, save, or invest your money in something else. It comes down to a question only you can answer. Do you choose to save to buy things you want or do you choose to buy those things today and end up paying more for them by using credit cards?

You can choose today to run your money and your life, not have your money run you. That process begins with thinking about your money, and thinking about money begins with setting a budget, or at least taking control of your money. Yes, "budgeting" is a dreaded word. And it can seem difficult because often what you spend varies from month to month; sometimes even the money you have coming in is different from month to month. Obstacles don't mean that you should not – and more important cannot – take control of your money. Here are some questions and answers that can help you with budgeting, credit cards, and beyond.

BUDGETING

Q: What is a budget and why do I need one, anyway?
A: A budget is a plan for spending and saving money. By tracking your money in and out, you can quickly see areas you can work on to improve your financial situation.

Q: When I think of doing a budget it seems overwhelming. Where do I start?
A: You can start by developing a budget from today forward. It's hard to go back in time and figure out where your money went, so just start by tracking where you spend your money for this next month. You can use our monthly budget worksheet (go to www.helpingyouinvest.com under the forms and documents tab) to show you how. You'll need to know how much you spend on food, gas, clothes, and how much you are saving. If you don't know this, the budget worksheet can help you figure out these expenses so you can begin to develop your monthly budget. At the end of the month you can sit down and see where your money went. Then you can focus on where you want to be spending your money – and even more important, where you want to be saving. It's easy: Just print out a budget worksheet and take just 15 minutes every day to write down where you spend; don't try to do your entire budget all at once. From here, you can develop a budget for what you will spend and save for in the next year.

Q: I have been working on a budget. Now that I have one how do I use it?
A: Use it to help you to continue to keep track of your expenses, which will help you spend within your means. A budget also helps you get where you want to go in life: Remember, it's not how much money you make, it's how much you spend. Reviewing your budget at the end of the month will help you determine if you are spending your money on things that are really, truly important to you. For example, you may find that you spent $400 for

the month dining out. You can then decide whether it's that important to you; if not, you can shift some of those dollars somewhere else. Money is simply a vehicle; it is all about putting your money toward what you value. Finally, remember that a budget is a work in progress and can change from year to year. Some expenses may go up from year to year such as the cost of electricity or gas for your car.

Q: I'm a single mom and am pressured every month when the bills arrive. I can barely make it month to month. Is there anything specific that I, as a single parent, should know?

A: It can be especially difficult to provide for a family on only one income but it's not impossible. It is important to be disciplined in order to make it work, so put together a strict budget so you can control your costs. That will force you to take a close look at where your money goes – and needs to go – each month. Commit yourself to stick to a budget so you are using the incoming funds adequately to pay for the necessary expenses. Keep an open mind so you recognize what is truly important: Make sure you are not only considering what needs to be paid for today, but also what savings you are going to need in the future.

Q: Our family wastes money going out to eat. How will eating in help us stay within our budget?

A: How many times would you say you and/or your family eat a meal at a restaurant? Once a week? Every other day? Every day? Keep track of how many times you go out to eat for one month and how much you're spending: On average, one dinner out for two people at a local casual restaurant costs about $30, compared to a dinner at home, which can run as low as $10. Now think: If you ate in just *one more time each month* you would save $20 a month on food, or $240 for the year. That's $240 more you could put away for your retirement or your children's college education, or a cabin. A night or two a month of a home-cooked meal (and it doesn't have to be fancy to taste good!) can help more than just your financial diet and your health.

Q: My husband and I are thinking that I should quit my job and stay home with our kids. How do I know if we can afford this?

A: With child care costs so expensive nowadays it may make more financial sense for you or your spouse to stay at home with the children. I have a number of clients whose day care costs them more than their mortgage every month. However, before you decide to quit, sit down with your spouse, weigh the pros and cons, and crunch the numbers. If one spouse stays at home, what will that do not only to your cash flow in the short term but to your retirement plan? If both spouses work, how will that affect your liabilities (your regular debts, like house payments or rent, utility bills, etc.) and your monthly budget? What about health-care coverage and other company benefits? Does one spouse have better and/or less-expensive health benefits than the other? Answering these questions will help you decide whether you can afford it, and who should stay home.

Q: My budget is really tight right now. I'm putting 15 percent of my paycheck into my 401(k). Is it OK if I cut back my 15 percent for a short time?

A: I don't recommend it. Once you lower the amount you're saving, it's hard to go back to your regular savings goal. You will also be missing out on the tax deduction you get by investing in your 401(k). See if you can cut back on other expenses before you cut back what you are saving; look at what you are spending on cable, your cell phone bill, and the extras like eating lunch out every day. Even important expenses such as life insurance or car insurance can sometimes be trimmed, so review those as well.

Q: How do I know if I'm spending too much? I just got another raise but I still don't feel like I am able to save much more. What do I do?

A: As your income rises, it's important to save more. It is all too easy to put more money into your house, car, and other activities, or buy things you've been wanting, instead of putting the money into savings. But once the paychecks stop – you retire, or are laid off, for example – you'll find it hard to maintain that lifestyle if you haven't saved appropriately. You want to use your raise to help you achieve your financial goals. When you start getting pay increases, consider putting more money into retirement savings. A little trick: Pretend you didn't get the raise. So if you got a 3 percent raise, take that 3 percent and have it automatically deposited into your 401(k); that way you won't even feel like it's "missing." You may need to also cut back on some of your lifestyle expenses so you can free up some cash to invest in order to reduce the chance of a severe cutback after you retire. Be aware of how much you are spending on your lifestyle, and make sure you're saving enough so you can continue the lifestyle you choose in the future.

Q: I just got engaged. My fiancée and I are both horrible with money and have little to save after we pay our bills. What should we do to save for a wedding?

A: It astounds me that the average cost of a wedding is $25,000. That's a lot of money. Imagine what you could do with the $25,000 as you start your life together. Your wedding day is a very special day and you want to re-member it for the rest of your life – but do you want to be paying for it for the rest of your life? It is still possible to have a beautiful and memorable wedding day without running up enormous debts. I would suggest setting a budget before you start planning your wedding so you only spend what you can afford. Think about how many people you want to invite; think about where you want the reception and how much you want to spend on food and beverages. When you have a budget set you start planning, you know exactly how much you can afford when ordering everything. Then figure out how much extra you have every month to save towards wedding costs and set up a savings or money market account that you put money in automatically every week or month. (You want a money market account or savings account so the money is liquid and accessible to you as you are making down payments on the wedding but also earning some interest on the money.) Again, it's not how much money you make, but how much you spend. Finally, remember: In the end, people may remember what a great party you threw, but what they'll really treasure is being there to see the happy looks on the bride's and groom's faces.

Q: I don't have any credit cards or any debt. I live on cash. Is this a bad thing?
A: Congratulations on being completely debt-free. However, in today's world, this could actually hurt you in the future. Without a credit card or any liabilities, you will not have a credit history; it is that history that lenders use to decide if they want to give you a loan. If you ever plan on buying a home, a car, or applying for a business or personal loan, you need the payment history that comes with owning, and using, a credit card. However, it's important to use credit cards wisely and to understand your credit. To establish a good credit history, get a major credit card. Then just make a few small purchases a month – you don't want to charge more than 30 to 50 percent of your credit limit each month. Then pay it off in full every month.

Q: My wife is spending my money and her money. She works, but wastes everything she earns (including what I earn at my job). She even gambles our money away. I am not sure if we are going to divorce, but I know she is going to leave me penniless if things keep up like this. What do I do?
A: First, you both need to look at your money not as just yours and hers, but as your money as a couple. Then you both can take control of your bud-

get and spending. Make a "money date" – it's one of the most important things you can do.

What's a money date? It's where you and your significant other get together at least once a month and talk about your money. On your first money date, you need to get on the same page. To start with, it helps to know that in most relationships, one person is a spender while the other a saver. If your significant other is a spender (which is what it sounds like), you need to find and develop some systems that work for you both to control the spending. Most of us don't recognize all the areas that we overspend – your wife may not quite realize it, either. Check out the budget worksheet on our website (www.helpingyouinvest.com) to track your expenses. Don't try to look backwards at where the money has gone; just go from today forward.

Then continue to have a "money date" at least once a month. You might also want to use this time to pay bills, but it could be just having a conversation about your investments, your liabilities, or your spending. The important thing is to keep discussing your money together.

Q: Do you have any tips on how I can keep my money in my hands? It just seems to disappear. I have a nice income but at the end of the month it is all gone.
A: It is imperative to keep track of your spending. Have you ever had a 10-20- or even 50-dollar bill in your pocket – then a few days (or maybe even hours) later, the money is gone, you have no idea what you spent it on, and you have nothing to show for it? For the next seven days – not the next six months or even the next thirty days, just *the next seven days* – carry around a notebook and write down *every single cent* that you spend. After those seven days, take a step back, look at what you spent your money on and see if those items fit your priorities. Then see if there is one area you could cut back on; if your spending is out of whack with your priorities, there probably is.

Q: I'm really bad about paying my bills on time. Do you have any suggestions?
A: Send in your payment a week to ten days before your bill is due so you
can avoid late fees. Also consider paying bills online and automatically. A
client of mine was recently paying her credit card bill, and they were going to charge her $14.95 if she made the payment online on the exact due
date; however, if she paid it three days earlier it was free. Set a time once
or twice a month when you know you are going to sit down and pay the
bills. Another tip: Make a spreadsheet with a list of all your bills; when you
pay them each month, write the dollar amount in. This way you not only
track your expenses, you also can make sure the bill is paid every month.
Paying your bills on time is more important than you might realize. You
not only avoid late fees, which nowadays run to $40 or more, but you also
help keep your credit score as high as possible. On top of that, it helps
to keep your interest rates low, because late payments on one card can
increase fees and interest rates on other cards as well.

Q: Can I post-date checks for a bill I need to pay?
A: You can, but there is no guarantee that the company will not run your
check until that date. It's happened to me. I was shopping once during February; I was a month ahead in my thinking, because March was a big month
– we were closing on a building for my business – so I accidentally wrote
the date on the check as March 18th, not February 18th and the store still
cashed the check. A better option is to pay the bill, seal the envelope; then
put a sticky note with the date of when to mail it, or write that in the box
where the postage stamp goes. Just make sure you mail it in enough time for
the company to receive the check before the due date.

Q: I use cash a lot and was wondering what to do with all the change I get?
A: Change is good, especially when you're trying to save money. Saving all
your change can add up. Every time you pay in cash, put any change in a

separate part of your wallet or purse. At the end of the day, put all that money into a special savings jar. I have had people try this for a month, and they come back to tell me they were able to save $30 to $60 a month. That works out to $360 to $720 a year – what an easy way to save money! So give it a try and see how much change you can collect this month. Remember, though, to take your change jar to the bank, credit union, or investment firm to deposit occasionally so you can earn interest on these dollars.

Q: I want to go on vacation, but my kids are asking to go on a more expensive vacation than I had planned for. Where do I start?
A: Unless you have the money for it, I don't recommend going over budget for this vacation. It's tough to say no to your kids, even when they're not your little ones anymore, and it's so easy to say "It's only a few hundred dollars more." But if you do this too often, you will end up spending over budget on lots of items, and things can get out of control. We want to have fun and travel, but there are other fun things to do that don't cost as much.

Q: I have all these expenses that I know I cannot cut back. Should I get a second job?
A: There is almost always an area you can cut back on. Do you have recurring expenses every month, such as a haircut? An easy way to cut some of these recurring costs can be to stretch the calendar a little more. Try adding a couple more weeks to the time between each appointment, so instead of getting a haircut every six weeks, try getting one every eight weeks (or more if you can handle it). At an average $50 per cut, that can save you $150 a year, sometimes more. Try looking at your calendar and see where else you can stretch the dates a little so you can save some money this year. However, if you find you just can't cut back enough, then you will have to either get a second job, find a job that pays more, or ask

for a raise. You can also make a little extra money by having a garage sale or selling some of your items you don't use online.

Q: I have been told I should have an emergency fund. What is this and how much should I have in that account?

A: Any financial advisor is going to recommend you have "**liquid money**" set aside that will cover three to six months of expenses. By liquid, I mean accessible: It is underneath your mattress, in your pocket, or, ideally, in some type of account where you earn interest, such as a money market account. Liquid money is for unexpected events that tap your pocketbook. For example, if you lose your job, you will need money to pay the mortgage and monthly bills until you can replace that lost income. In the case of a car accident, you will need liquid dollars to cover car repair and possibly some medical expenses. It might make it easier if you don't focus too much on the number of months – think more about the dollar amount so you know how much you need to set aside so you can sleep at night. Ideally, this money is immediately accessible, of course, but you also want to earn as much interest as you can. Money market accounts are more liquid than CDs (certificates of deposits) and typically pay more interest than savings accounts. Account services vary, however, so shop around for rates, fees, and services.

Money Tip:

Make sure you have three to six months worth of income set aside in liquid money.

Q: What is a money market account?
A: A money market account is a savings account in high gear – that is, you typically earn more interest in a money market account than in a basic savings account. Most money market accounts are insured up to $100,000, some up to $1 million. A money market account is invested in CDs and short-term bonds from the government, not in the more volatile stock market. Although money market accounts are typically good places to keep liquid money, some have restrictions, such as a higher balance requirement, and/or limited withdrawals per month or year, so make sure you research the details.

Q: I have a lot of debt and don't know where to start. I am overwhelmed and frustrated. What is the first step I should take?
A: The first step is to gather all of your financial information. You want to know how much debt you have and the interest rate on each mortgage, credit card, student loan, etc. When looking at saving for the future, it is important to get rid of debt. Then stop using your credit cards; if you have credit cards you can't pay off in full every month you are living beyond your means and you will want to make a budget for yourself. You may want to look at consolidating any credit card debt you may have. Consolidating your credit card debt is taking all the credit cards that you have a balance on and merging them – transferring all the balances – to one card (preferably with a lower interest rate). If you are a homeowner, you may want to take out a home equity loan or line of credit, because the interest rate may be lower than your credit card, and any interest paid is tax deductible. Be careful if you do this though, because you are now attaching credit card debt to your house and if you don't make the payments you could lose your home.

Once you have analyzed your debt, you can start to pay it off, either by consolidation or one loan at a time. Start by paying the most money to the account with the highest interest. For example, you have three credit cards. One card is charging you 6 percent and you owe $5,000, the second card is charging you 15 percent and you owe $1,000, and the third credit card is charging you 22 percent and you owe $2,000; in this case, you would pay the most you can to the third credit card, with the 22 percent interest rate. You then make the minimum payments to the other two cards. Once the 22 percent card is paid off, take the money you were putting towards that card and start paying more on the 15 percent interest card; and so on. If you are committed to whittling away your debt this way, pretty soon you will start to see it shrink.

Q: I'm looking at going back to school but realize I would need to take out some loans. Is this OK?

A: There is good debt and bad debt. Good debt is OK: a mortgage, student loan or something that is an investment in you. Bad debt is basically anything else – credit cards, personal loans, etc. However, when you take out loans for school you may be offered more money than you truly need for school expenses. Don't be tempted; you don't want to use this money to help keep up your standard of living. Student loans are for school.

Q: We have many credit cards (some with high interest rates), a home mortgage, a home equity loan and a car payment. I would like to get rid of the credit card debt, but we just don't make enough money to make a dent in it. I have thought about either transferring to a lower-interest card or getting a consolidation loan and getting rid of all but one card for emergencies. What is the best way to get rid of the debt the fastest?

A: Run your credit report and get some budgeting help. The way to get rid of debt is first to see where the debt is coming from, and if you are still accumulating debt to stop it from piling up even more. Once that's done you can change your future spending to help limit any further increase in debt. The next goal is to pay as much as you can on the highest-interest card or debt; once that debt is paid off, start working on the next-highest interest. Getting out of debt usually only works when you change your behavior. If you have debt and are living beyond your means, you need to look at why you have debt and if the debt truly fits your larger priorities in life.

Q: I get a HUGE tax refund back every year, and I'm wondering how I should invest the money?

A: Getting a huge refund back every year is *not* a good thing. If you have a refund every year, this means you are giving the government an interest free-loan. It's better to have a larger paycheck every month and use the money throughout the year to spend, save or invest. Uncle Sam does not pay you anything to use your money, and if you are using credit cards and you're being charged interest, this can dramatically hurt your financial situation; meanwhile, you're getting no benefits from Uncle Sam. For now, take the refund and pay off any credit card debt, fund your Traditional or Roth IRA, or put the money in a money market account to build some liquid money. Then change your withholding to minimize your refund next year.

YOUR HOUSE, YOUR CAR

Q: I am considering buying my first house. How do I know that I can really afford to own a home?

A: Buying a house is a big deal, so don't make the decision without careful consideration of the costs and benefits to you. When you're figuring out the amount you can afford, you need to consider several other factors besides just the mortgage payment. Among the top considerations are how much of a down payment you can afford. It is possible in some cases to buy a house with zero down; however, the additional costs that might be associated with this might not be worth it. You also need to consider the expenses that are going to go along with owning a home.

Q: Are there any hidden costs associated with buying a home?

A: You're right to realize there are other costs you might incur besides just the mortgage payment, closing fees, other commissions you may pay to a real estate agent, and any other costs of the actual purchase. You don't want to do all you can to buy a house, then move in and have no money for a bed to sleep in or a couch to sit on. Some other expenses you want to factor in are insurance and taxes, which you will have to pay yearly, plus maintenance and improvement costs. You might assume you'll encounter these costs when you first move in, but remember, they may recur over the years as well.

Q: What is PMI?

A: PMI is private mortgage insurance. It is required when you don't put at least 20 percent down on your property. It's money you have to pay each month that is just wasted, so when you buy a house, you want to put at least 20 percent down. If you don't have enough to make a 20 percent down payment you should consider waiting until you have enough so that you can truly afford your home. Most mortgage companies require that you live in the house for at least two years before you can consider getting rid of the PMI payment, even if you have 20 percent equity in the house because of appreciation, debt repayment, or improvements in the home.

Q: Recently I had damage to my home that was not covered by insurance. I am trying to figure out how to pay for it because I don't have enough in savings or enough equity in my home. I feel like I have two options: Put it on a credit card or take money from my Roth IRA. What do I do?

A: First off, cashing in retirement accounts to help supplement your lifestyle is not smart; that includes taking a loan on your 401(k), which is the ultimate last resort. You may be able to use some of the equity in your house, then use your credit card or a loan to cover the rest. Depending on the damage, you may be able to put off repairs until you have saved up enough money to pay for them outright. This is yet another reason it's so important to have liquid money set aside for unexpected events.

Q: I'm wondering if I should rush to pay off my mortgage?

A: Paying off a mortgage is obviously a great way to eliminate debt, but you need to take a hard look at the numbers. If you have a great interest rate you generally don't need to; all the interest you pay on your mortgage could be deductible. And if you have a low-interest mortgage, you should usually first focus on maxing out retirement plans before paying extra on your mortgage; it's better to get rid of any high-interest debt first.

If your mortgage interest rate is much higher than what you could make by investing the money within the same time period, though, it's a good idea to pay it off. Also, having equity in your home allows you to set up a home equity line of credit, which is a way to access cash in case of an emergency.

Q: I'm thinking of taking out a home equity loan to pay off some credit cards. Is this OK?

A: Be cautious. First, find out how this kind of loan may affect you. Home equity loans reduce or may even eliminate the equity you have built up in your home. "Equity" means the cash you would have if you sold your house and paid off your mortgage loans; if you can't make payments on your home equity loan, you could lose your home. Be sure to consider the interest rate available for the loan, along with any associated fees. The loan could also affect your credit score. Finally, make sure that if you use your house to pay off your credit cards you don't continue to use the credit cards to run up even more debt.

Q: What is the difference between a home equity line of credit and a home equity loan?

A: A **home equity *loan*** is a certain dollar amount with a fixed interest rate, whereas a **home equity *line*** often has a variable interest rate with a flexible dollar amount, up to a specified amount. The interest on either is tax-deductible.

Q: Which is better, a home equity line of credit or a home equity loan?

A: It depends on what you're looking for. If you want flexibility, the line might be a better option. If you want a set payment and a steady interest rate, a loan may be better. Home equity lines are flexible, but the interest rate can vary, which means your payments could go up over time. A home equity loan is at a fixed rate and a specific dollar amount, so it's great if you will need a specified amount, say, $40,000 for a home project. Some home equity lines of credit give you checks off the account, which is nice when you are doing remodeling projects and need money but not all at once. Home equity lines are great if you need flexibility or to use in case of an emergency.

Q: What is an ARM?

A: ARM stands for adjustable rate mortgage. This means that your house payments can vary from year to year depending on what kind of ARM you have. Some ARMs adjust every year, some every three or five. An ARM can be a good fit under some circumstances but if you plan to stay in a house for a long time – usually five years or more – generally you want to take a good look at a fifteen- to thirty-year conventional mortgage. Not only could you lock in at a lower rate, but you won't have to worry about your housing costs spiraling out of control.

Q: I am looking at refinancing my home. How do I know that the company I am working with is reputable and one that I can trust?

A: The signs of a disreputable company are one that:

- Encourages you to falsify your application to get the loan.
- Urges you to borrow more than you need.
- Pushes you to accept payment terms that you cannot realistically meet.
- Fails to give you the required disclosures (APR, rescission rights, etc.).
- Shows up at closing with a different loan product than you agreed to.
- Asks you to sign blank forms. ("It will speed things up. We will fill in the blanks later, trust me.")
- Denies you copies of documents you signed.

Any one of these signals should make you leery of the company. There are plenty of trustworthy companies out there that will help you. Do your research and be skeptical of a company that has even some of these warning signals.

Q: I am looking at buying a new car. Is it better to lease or buy?

A: Buying is typically the better option. First, make sure that you can afford the car, not just the payment per month. So often I see people just focusing on the monthly payment, and not the true and total cost of the vehicle. Yes, maybe it's "only" a $400-a-month payment, but if it's a five- or seven-year loan, it might be a car they can't afford. You want to look at the cost of the car, not the payment – does the vehicle cost $20,000 or $40,000? You also have to consider other costs such as insurance and maintenance. Cars are a depreciating asset – that is, what the car is worth drops with every passing day you own the car. If you lease a vehicle, you will always have a new car, but you will always have a payment and never own anything. You are signing a contract, and you have mileage, maintenance, and care stipulations that could end up costing you a lot of money. I have had many clients that have leased vehicles and driven many more miles than they were allotted in the lease so they had extreme penalties and charges just to get rid of the car.

Q: What does it mean to be upside-down on a vehicle?

A: Being upside-down on a vehicle is, alas, not lying on your back on the hood gazing up into the sky; it is owing more on the vehicle than it is actually worth. Let's say you could get $5,000 for your vehicle if you sold it, but you owe $9,000 on a car loan. You have a liability, not an asset. This usually happens when you take out a five- to seven-year loan on a vehicle. To help ensure you don't get upside-down in your vehicle, only buy one you can afford to pay off quickly; a two- to four-year loan is about the longest you should have. Remember, a vehicle is a depreciating asset and loses value quickly.

Q: I'm looking at buying a new car, but they're so expensive. To afford the monthly payments I'd have to get a longer-term loan (about five years). Is this OK?

A: About 40 percent of buyers of new vehicles owe more on their car than it is worth. One cause of this is because they're using a longer- term loan. If something unexpected happened and you had to trade in or sell your car, you might still be left with debt from the original loan. To avoid this, make sure you don't trade in a car until you have it completely paid off or it is worth more than you owe. And don't buy a car until you can pay it off in four to five years. Consider driving these cars longer – at least seven years. Also consider buying a used vehicle. These measures will help you owe less and get your car paid off a lot faster.

Q: I need a new car and I'm not sure I can afford the one I would like. How can I figure out if I can truly afford this more expensive car?

A: If you want to buy a brand-new car, a house, or any other item that would increase your monthly payments, take six months and pretend that you already owned the item. For a brand-new car, for example, think about the $500 monthly payment. Every month, actually write out a check for $500 but make it payable to yourself; then put it in an envelope and put it in a drawer. After six months, take a step back and see how it feels. Can you truly afford that car? This exercise will help you realize whether you can afford it or you need to look for a less expensive car. If you decide that the $500 a month is too much to handle right now, then you'll have even more of a down payment set aside for the car when you are financially ready.

CREDIT CARDS AND SCORES

Q: I love credit cards. Do you have any suggestions to help me?

A: Yes. Take a glass of water, put your credit card in the glass, and put the glass of water (with the card still in it!) in the freezer. Then the next time you want to use your credit card, you'll need to take the glass out of the freezer and wait for the ice to thaw before you can actually use the card. This forces you to think differently about how much you really "have to" have something and when you have to have it, and it should help you change your behavior about spending money. If you are not able to immediately pull out your credit card for that next impulse purchase, you will likely save yourself some money – and you'll also probably be spending your money on your true needs rather than just your wants.

Q: What makes up your credit score?

A: Your **credit score** is like your report card, with a grade on how responsible you are with your money. The score is made up of how much your income is compared with what you owe, your history of making payments on time and using credit, how much debt you have, and a variety of other factors. Your credit score follows your Social Security number. If you are married, you and your spouse each have your own credit score, but joint liabilities with your spouse (or anyone else), such as a mortgage with both your names on it, can affect your credit score as well.

Q: Is credit only with my husband or do we each have our own credit?

A: You each have your own credit score; it follows your Social Security number. It is especially important for women to make sure they have credit under their own name. A number of years ago I bought a new car. I was told that my car and loan would go into my husband's name because he had better credit. I couldn't believe it – I never carried credit card debt, always paid my bills on time, and had never bounced a check in my life! What I realized is that once women get married, often their husband's name goes first on just about everything: credit cards, mortgage, electric bill, etc. – or worse, only his name goes on those items. If you don't have a checking account, money market savings account, or credit card, consider getting one – in your name. Take the credit card and charge your gas on the card once a month; then every month pay that bill in full to establish a good credit score.

Q: What is a good credit score?

A: Credit scores generally range from 500 to 850. The higher your score, the better your credit and the better the rate you'll get the next time you take out a loan. Your score is important; what makes up your score is what's on your credit report so make sure all that information is correct and you stay on top of your credit.

Q: I am looking at buying a house and was told I have a credit score of 730. What does this mean?

A: A score of 730 would mean that you have relatively good credit. Your credit score is one of the most important numbers you have. You need a good score to get a great rate on a loan; sometimes potential employers also look at your credit, so it is important to check it so you can fix any errors. You should be able to receive one credit report at no charge per year from the three credit reporting agencies: Equifax, TransUnion or Experian.

Q: Where do I get a free copy of my credit report?

A: The only free website where you can get a free copy of your **credit report** is www.annualcreditreport.com. Don't rely on an Internet search – many sites state they are free but are not. However, the site I listed does not give you your credit **score** (as opposed to the report) – you need to pay a little extra for that. You should run your credit report at least once a year to stay on top of your credit. Look for errors and make sure that your credit score stays high; if it's less than what you'd like, be aware of how you can raise your score. The three credit bureaus – Equifax, Experian, and TransUnion – each will give you one free report every year through this website. You should do this; so, for example, today you can go to the site and get the report from Experian. Then three to four months from now you go to www.annualcreditreport.com and pull the one from TransUnion. Three to four months after that you can pull the one for free once a year from Equifax.

Q: How quickly can my credit score improve and what can I do to improve it?

A: Generally it takes at least six to twelve months to start to improve your credit score. You can help your credit score by getting a credit card, charging a small amount on it every month, and paying it off in full every billing period. You can also help by keeping a balance below 30 to 50 percent of your credit limit on each card. Also, pay your bills on time: If you are late on one payment with one card that can affect other cards that you own.

Q: How do I get bad things off my credit report?

A: You can dispute any incorrect information with the credit bureaus themselves. If you have some debt you did not pay listed on your report, generally it will take seven to ten years before it comes off. Inaccurate information, however, such as reported late payments that you disagree with or a listing for a debt that is not yours is repairable. If you have more than one item you are disputing, then you may have to send a separate letter for each instance to be certain that each item is addressed.

It's important to make sure all the information on your credit report is correct; on top of that, each report is not uniform from company to company, so make sure you have them from all three agencies.

Once you have your credit reports, verify all the information. You may have accounts that are reported incorrectly or that have a wrong name or address. Every report is also scored. Scoring is the system that creditors use to determine your credit experience. These scores are valid for all three agencies and are uniform in value. If you look at all the information on your credit report and it is correct but the score is low, then you are going to have to either improve your payment history or reduce your debt.

Q: I have about eleven credit cards that I don't use. Should I close these accounts?

A: Yes – having too much available credit can lower your credit score. But don't close them all; just close the accounts that you don't use. Leave open a few cards that you have had for a long time; these give you a "**credit history**," which will make up part of your credit score. (Make sure on your credit report these cards show your history of paying your bills on time and paying in full, though.) When you close accounts, make sure that you show that you, the consumer, closed them, and get a confirmation mailed to you from the credit card company so that it shows up correctly on your credit report.

Q: Is it OK to take advantage of the zero percent-interest credit card offers that are out there?

A: Zero percent offers are great and you can use them to your advantage, but they can also dramatically hurt your credit and your wallet if not used correctly. Look at the fine print and know the type of contract you are getting into; credit card companies are in the business to make money and they sure don't make it by offering zero percent. If you decide to take up such an offer, make sure you pay off the balance *in full* by the expiration date of the specific offer. If not, all that back interest could be immediately charged to you.

Q: I get a bunch of credit card solicitations in the mail. Does this hurt my credit score?

A: No. Credit card solicitations in the mail don't hurt your score unless you take action on the solicitations.

Q: We paid off our car loan, but it still shows up on our credit report. What do we do?

A: Nothing. Typically, accounts you have paid or closed will stay on your credit report; in fact, this is a good thing because it shows you paid your balance in full. If you have an old car loan that shows up on your credit report as *un*paid, first contact your loan provider to ensure that it has been paid. Then contact the credit reporting agency to dispute the incorrect information on your credit report.

Q: Is it OK to take a cash advance from a credit card?

A: Generally no. For one thing, your interest rate for the advance is going to be higher than for regular purchases. To make it even worse, when you make a payment your money will first go against the purchases you have made on your card. *Only when those are paid off* will it go to pay for any cash advances. So let's say you're paying 9.9 percent on your purchases. Your payment first goes against that 9.9 percent, and *then* the 22 percent interest you are paying on cash advances, so it's a double whammy.

Q: When I get my credit card bills in the mail every month I'm usually shocked at the balance. What can I do?

A: Track what you spend. What do you do with your extra check registers? A great way to use them is with your credit card, to write down what you're using your credit card on. Then make sure that your credit card bill is correct and you are not being overcharged – and not shocked when your bill arrives.

Q: I have three store credit cards that I don't want anymore. Should I just shred the cards? Or is it better to shred these cards *and* close the accounts?

A: Generally you don't want to shred a card without closing the account. Make sure you ask for a confirmation letter stating that you, the consumer, closed the account because you wanted to, not because there was a problem. You want to make sure that your credit report has been corrected because any bad or wrong information could affect your credit score and you want to have the highest credit score possible.

Q: I just bought a house and don't have a credit card. Should I get one?

A: Yes. You'll want it in case of emergencies and it will help build your credit. Get a major credit card (not just a store card) and charge something small on it every month. Then be sure to pay off the card in full and on time every month. However, if you just bought a house, you may want to wait a few months. If you have too many inquiries into your credit in a short period this can drop your credit score as well.

Q: I have a $40,000 home equity loan, about $5,000 in a car loan, and $2,000 in credit card debt. Is this bad?
A: In your situation I would focus on getting rid of the $2,000 credit card first, then focus on the car loan, then the home equity line of credit last. The reason is the credit card loan is probably the highest interest rate and the home equity loan of credit is probably the lowest, plus the interest is deductible on the home equity loan if you qualify.

Q: I have $15,000 of credit card debt and I am wondering if it is smart to refinance my house or to get a home equity loan to pay off my debt?
A: There is nothing wrong with doing this as long as you stop using the credit cards so you don't go further in debt. It's important to know that credit card debt is "unsecured debt," whereas housing debt is "secured debt." Unsecured debt is not attached to anything; secured debt is a car loan that is attached to your car, or a mortgage that is attached to your house. This means in practical terms that if you can't pay your home equity loan you could lose your house, so evaluate whether you can afford the payments – you don't want to risk losing your house to pay off the credit card debt. But you may be able to get a lower interest rate and possibly deduct the interest.

IDENTITY THEFT

Q: I know a number of co-workers who've been victims of identity theft. What can I do to do protect myself?

A: A few simple measures to help prevent identity theft and fraud:

- Don't carry your Social Security card with you; memorize the number instead.
- Shred your financial records, credit card bills, statements, or any personal information rather than just tossing them in the garbage.
- Never leave a gas station or ATM receipt behind.
- Don't give out your personal information unless it is to someone you know and trust.
- Copy the front and back of your credit cards and file the information in a safe place.
- Put your purse, laptop, or any other important personal items in the trunk of your car before you leave for your destination.
- Last but not least, make sure you watch your mailbox. Collect your mail quickly and consider dropping off your mail directly at the post office rather than leaving in your door for mail carrier (or identity thief!) to pick up.

You can be your own watchdog by running your credit report quarterly, shredding old financial documents, and staying on top of your credit.

Q: How can I keep my Social Security number safe?

A: First, you should NEVER carry your Social Security card or Social Security number with you. If you have one in your wallet right now (or even one of your kid's cards or their numbers) take it out. Also, copy the back and front of your credit cards and keep the copies in a secure place separate from where you keep your Social Security card.

Q: I received a call asking me for personal information over the phone. Is it safe to give out this information?

A: Be cautious and aware of who you are talking to. Don't give any important information such as credit card numbers or Social Security numbers to any person or company that you do not completely trust. This is especially true over the phone. You can always ask the person for their phone number and call them back; you want to verify the company and the person you are calling. If it is not a company you have accounts with or a place you would like to do business with I wouldn't give out any personal information. Some people only give out information to people or organizations they have initiated contact with. The same is true with random e-mail solicitations. The IRS or your credit card company or your bank are not going to e-mail you to verify your personal information.

Q: I need to hire a housekeeper. How do I know this person will not steal my identity and ruin me financially?

A: In-home workers have been implicated in a good chunk of identity theft, so it pays to know and check the people you let through your door. Try to get references from friends and colleagues. Information that applicants should willingly supply includes the names and numbers of their past three employers, and their own addresses for the past ten years. Other information you'll want to know is whether they've used any other names (including maiden names), any history of alcohol and drug use, or any run-ins with the law. You can find this information by doing a background check and running their credit report. There are many online services you can use to help you run a background check and their credit reports. You can also check with your local police department. When interviewing, ask your applicants what frustrated them most about their past jobs and how they dealt with that frustration.

Q: Should I opt out of credit card solicitations? Will this help protect my credit?

A: You sure can. Go to www.optoutprescreen.com to help to eliminate the solicitations that you get in the mail and e-mail. The most important step you can take is to shred any solicitations that you do get in the mail before you dispose of them; otherwise your personal information could get into the hands of someone you don't know.

Q: When should I freeze my credit?

A: If you have been the victim of identity theft, you can freeze your credit for free. I would freeze your credit if you have been a victim of identity theft or you are suspect that someone has the ability to compromise your identity or your credit, for example if your purse was lost or stolen. The best measures are preventive. For some tips on how to protect yourself, see the first question in this section.

CHAPTER 2

INVESTING 101

Once you have a budget and can save money, you can start investing your money. There's a difference between investing and saving. Investing is putting your money into investment vehicles that could have greater growth potential. You are putting this money away generally for the longer term and/or taking on more risk. Saving is just putting money away, such as in a money market account. It's technically "lazy" money. We all work hard for our money so it's important to make your money work hard for you.

This chapter barely scratches the surface of investing basics because there are so many things to invest in, but keep in mind the overall point is to invest your money so you can reach your financial goals and dreams. I encourage you to seek out a financial advisor to help you with your own specific situation. Most financial advisors offer a free initial consultation or workshops you can attend, so there's no reason not call them and meet with them. Here are a few of the common questions about investing that will give few ideas to get started.

GETTING STARTED

Q: What are some common mistakes people make with their money?
A: Not having enough liquid money. This money is for unexpected events that tap your pocket book. For example, if you lose your job, you will need money to pay the mortgage and monthly bills until you can replace that income. Or if there were a car accident, you would need liquid dollars to cover car repair and medical expenses. Other mistakes are not maxing out work retirement plans and IRAs and using credit cards to fund a life-style you cannot afford.

Q: Is there a minimum I need to start investing?
A: There is a big misperception that you have to have a lot of money to invest, but as I've said before, it's not how much you make but how much you spend and save. It's true that some investments do have minimums, ranging from $1,000 to $100,000, but with most financial advisors, you can set up an account to start saving monthly with just the commitment that you will have money automatically withheld from your checking or savings account every month, sometimes as little as $25 a month.

The hardest part is taking the first step and opening an account to get the money out of your hands every month, but think of it this way: Instead of having lunch out every day with your friends, cut back to only several times a month. You'll likely save close to $10 a day; and did you that know that $10 a day for twenty-five years at an 8 percent rate of return could add up to over $270,000? That's an expensive lunch with your friends.

Q: How much does it cost to invest?
A: It depends on what you're investing in. Some investments are more expensive than others; there are the costs of buying and selling the invest-ment, and you could also incur the cost of professional advice. Some other

fees such as investment management fees, trading fees, or annual fees to have an account may also come into play. It's important to understand what you're getting for what you're paying, but realize that fees are relative. I would rather own an investment that returns 15 percent and costs me 2 percent than own an investment with a 6 percent return that costs me 1 percent.

Q: When is the right time to invest?
A: My clients sometimes ask me, "Have we hit the bottom yet?" My response is always the same: I know better than to try to time the market; it's virtually impossible. Successful investing is about time in the market, and there is no time like the present to invest. You, the investor, should be committed to continue investing regardless of whatever market fluctuations or life situations are going on around you at the time.

Money Tip:

If you have investment accounts all over consolidate your accounts so you have one asset allocation.

Q: I have been trying to organize my finances. My money is spread around with a number of different companies. I have pulled all of my statements together but still don't know what I have. Can you help?
A: Yes. You have taken the first step of pulling all of your account statements together. Write down all of your assets then subtract all your liabilities – this is how you calculate your net worth. (Assets are all the things you own; liabilities are all the places you owe. In general, something you consume is *not* considered an asset.) After completing

these steps, figure out what your financial goals are and write them down. The next step now is to have a plan. At this point, you're ready to sit down with a financial advisor who can help you with that plan to help you meet your goals.

Q: I have heard many financial advisors talk about the "time value" of money. This term flies right over my head. What does it mean?
A: Time value is the concept that money available today is worth more than the same amount in the future – the longer you have your money grow and compound, the faster your money accumulates.

How can that be? A dollar is a dollar, isn't it? Yes, but a dollar in hand today can be invested so that it grows in value over time. From this it follows that the earlier you start investing the easier it is. For example, if you go out today and spend $45 on a new pair of shoes your cost of buying a new pair of shoes is not just the price of the shoes but also the time and cost of what else you could have done with your time and your money.

Q: What is inflation?
A: Inflation is the silent killer of money. Inflation means that things get more expensive as time goes on; as we go about our day-to-day activities, inflation is rising at about two to 4 percent a year. Do you remember 1999? Back then it only cost us 32 cents to mail a letter; now look at where prices are! Think back even further – in the 1960s you could buy a house for what it now costs you to buy a car. Imagine how inflation will affect you after thirty years or more.

The best way to beat inflation is to "diversify," which is to put your money in a number of different types of investments and rebalance those assets from time to time. Stocks in particular have historically outpaced inflation over the long term.

Q: I have about $122,000 sitting in my checking account and am not sure what I should be doing with it. I would like this to be relatively liquid because I want to use it eventually for a down payment on a house. Does this make sense?

A: It does not make sense not to earn the most interest that you can. Having a large amount of money in a checking account, which has a very low and sometimes no rate of return, is actually losing you money because of inflation. You may want to look at putting some of the money away for the long term or look at money market accounts or possibly a CD or two to earn the most interest. To keep the money completely liquid your best bet is a money market account. This money is accessible to you if you need it, but you are earning more interest on your dollars than you would in a checking account.

Q: What does it mean when interest rates go up?

A: Think of balancing interest rates and your money like a teeter-totter. As interest rates go up, bonds go down. But also keep an eye on your credit cards, lines of credit, or other liabilities that may have an interest rate that fluctuates. If interest rises, that can be good for accounts that earn money based on varying interest rates; but if it's also tied to how much you pay on your liabilities, you will pay more interest on your debts.

Q: My greatest fear is to end up as a bag lady. What can I do?

A: First, you can change how you think about money. Money is not your enemy; it is simply a vehicle to help you get where you want to go. Second, make sure you are taking advantage of all types of accounts that are available such as a Roth IRA, 401(k)s, money market accounts, 529 plans, etc. The third thing you can do is enlist the help of a financial advisor to help you develop a plan for your future. Then all you need to do is focus on what you need to do to implement your plan rather than focusing on your fears.

Q: Are there differences between men and women when it comes to investing?
A: Yes. Men and women are often different in how they use money, how they feel about it, and how they communicate about money. First of all, in most relationships one partner will be the spender and one will be the saver. While this is not necessarily linked to whether you're a man or woman – it depends more on how you were raised about money and your personality – it's important to understand the differences and take the positives of both personalities to make the most of your money and your relationship. Then set time aside each month to have a "money date." Use this time to understand and appreciate how you and your spouse view money. Discuss your monthly spending and saving. Review your goals, dreams, and desires for you financial plans.

Now, to the differences: Women typically live longer than men, by an average of seven years. They make less money overall over their lifetimes due to childbearing and family responsibilities. If they have children, they are out of the workforce an average of 11½ years; this is 11½ years that women do not have money going into a retirement plan or Social Security. And they earn lower wages (an average of 30 percent less) than men. Lower wages mean smaller pensions and Social Security payments. Divorce or legal separation also can complicate women's financial futures. A general rule is that men should be saving 10 percent of their income towards retirement and women should be saving 12 percent.

As a woman, I also firmly believe that it costs us more to live than men. Have you ever compared the cost of getting your haircut versus the haircut of a man? What about dry cleaning? Men's shirts are $1.89 if I drop them off before noon; mine are $4 (and if they're silk, even more). These can be hard costs for women to cut, but one area you can look at cutting back in is the money you spend eating out. If you bring your lunch to work rather than eating out every day this can make a dramatic difference – did you know that saving $7 every day for forty-two years at a 10 percent rate of return will add up to over $1.3 million? Yes, $1.3 *million*. Past performance is no guarantee of future results.

TYPES OF INVESTMENTS

Q: What is a CD?

A: CD stands for certificate of deposit. You are lending the bank a certain amount of money for a specific period, and they guarantee you a certain percentage return. CDs are low-risk, but also low-return investments. Some advantages:

Your money is safe. The FDIC protects your money up to $100,000, and sometimes the Securities Investors Protection Corporation (SIPC) will protect it for even more.

They are fixed-rate investments. The rate might be very low, but you at least know exactly what you will get in the future.

A disadvantage: You could pay a penalty for early withdrawal, so the money may not be as liquid as you need. There is also reinvestment risk when your CD is due; in other words, interest rates may be lower than expected when you go to reinvest your money after your CD comes due.

Q: I was told I should invest in an annuity. What is this?

A: An annuity is a form of contract sold by life insurance companies that guarantees a payment to the "annuitant" (the person who owns the annuity) at some time in the future. This guarantee is based on the claims-paying ability of the insurance company. There are two main types of annuities: fixed and variable. Fixed annuities are those that earn a set rate on the money that is invested. With a variable annuity, the money is invested according to the decision you and your financial advisor make; it can be invested more in the stock market and have a rate that goes up and down.

Q: What are the advantages of an annuity?

A: I see a few main reasons people get into annuities. Annuities grow tax-deferred, so you don't have to pay taxes every single year on the money. I also see people purchasing an annuity if they want to protect their principal or if they want to have a fixed monthly payment. Talk to your financial advisor to see if this fits your situation.

Q: Should I invest in real estate?

A: Investing in real estate goes well beyond buying a home; we all need a place to live, but I don't classify home ownership as investing. In fact, did you know that there are twenty-two different types of real estate?

If it makes sense for your allocation to add real estate, you may want to look at a REIT. A REIT stands for real estate investment trust; it lets you invest in real estate as part of a group. The trust owns a variety of buildings and various different types of real estate – you as an individual don't own one particular building. Instead, you own pieces of a lot of different types of real estate. Investing in real estate, or REITs, involves special risks such as potential illiquidity (your money is not accessible), and may not be suitable for all investors. There is also no assurance the investment objectives of this program will be attained.

STOCKS

Q: What is a stock dividend?

A: John D. Rockefeller once said, "Do you know the only thing that gives me pleasure? It's to see my dividends coming in." Not coincidentally, Rockefeller was reportedly the richest man in the world when he retired. If you own stock in a company, the company may decide to take some of its profits and rather than investing further in the company, to give money back to you in the form of a dividend. The company's board of directors decides if it will declare a dividend, how often it will declare it, and the dates associated with the dividend. Quarterly payment of dividends is very common, annually or semiannually is less common, and many companies don't pay dividends at all.

Q: What does it means if the market is a bull or a bear?

A: This is common terminology to explain how the market is doing. A bear market is an extended period – generally more than a year – when prices in the market are declining. It is often measured by a percentage decline of more than 20 percent. A bull market is a long period when prices in the market are generally increasing. Bull markets occur when roughly 80 percent of all stocks advance – that is, their price goes up – over an extended period.

Q: How can I find information on a privately traded company?

A: A company that is private is not available to be purchased on the stock exchange. A public company is one that is owned by shareholders, and you can buy shares and become a shareholder relatively easily. It's hard to find a lot of information on companies that aren't public and they can be a riskier investment if the company is very small. Private companies are not required to issue annual reports, but you can call the investor relations department, which can give you any information available to the public. You can also look at their financial statements, if the company is willing to share that information with you.

Q: My friend keeps bragging to me about the stocks he has made money in. Should I take some of his advice and buy some of the stocks he owns?

A: Usually by the time you get the "recommendation" it is too late. I call this the "water cooler theory." Plenty of people you know will tell you about all the money they made on their recent stock purchases – but do those same individuals ever tell you about how much money they lost on their investments as well? It's important to invest for the long term rather than trying to make money in the short term from a "hot tip." The whole goal is to buy low, hold onto those investments, then sell them at a high price years down the road.

Q: When is it a good time to sell a stock that has had a loss in your account?

A: Sometimes selling a stock that has suffered a loss can be a great strategy for turning a bad investment into a smart tax break. In a taxable account, your losses can offset capital gains; you can write off up to $3,000 a year as a loss on your taxes. So if you are holding a stock that has been underperforming in your taxable account, you should consider selling it and offsetting the loss with gains from your other investments. If you change your mind, you can always buy the asset back after thirty days.

> **Money Tip:**
>
> Watch your stock holdings. You generally don't want more than 5–10% of your net worth in any one stock at any one time.

Q: How much money should I invest in stocks?

A: The amount of money you should have in stocks (also called "equities," not to be confused with the "equity" in your house) depends on several things, including your investment time frame, how comfortable you are with short-term market volatility, and even your age.

Q: Is it safe to invest in the stock market?

A: It certainly can be, but it is virtually impossible to time the market. Remember, successful investing isn't about timing the market, it's about *time in the market*, and there is no time like the present to invest. In fact, there are a number of strategies to consider during long periods of market volatility, when the stock market seems to be on a roller-coaster. Two common strategies are dollar-cost averaging and diversification. **Dollar-cost averaging** is perhaps the most time-tested way to invest. It means investing regularly in both up and down markets. In practical terms, that means you buy more shares when the price is low and fewer shares when the price is high. Such a plan involves continuous investment of the same amount of money in securities, regardless of changes in price. (Investors should consider their ability to continue purchasing through periods of low price levels. Such a plan does not assure a profit and does not protect against loss in declining markets.) **Diversification** is another often recommended strategy. If your portfolio is down more than the average (you're not making as much money on your investments as the average earnings in the market), perhaps you are over-concentrated in a particular asset class, such as internationally or in small companies. This can increase overall risk. Diversification is having your money in a variety of asset classes – in other words, not putting put all your eggs in one basket.

Q: How can I weather the ups and downs of the stock market without going crazy?

A: The longer I'm in this business as a financial advisor, the more convinced I am that change is the only constant. I realize that market ups and downs can be extreme and unpredictable, and that volatility can wreak havoc on your nerves. It's times like these that I like to remind my clients to expect the unexpected and try not to let emotion derail their long-term investment plans. One of the most common temptations is to lose patience and sell as prices continue to drop. Don't. But it may be a good time to re-evaluate your portfolio and to assess your situation. Once you make an assessment you can determine if you need to make any changes. And while I don't have a crystal ball, I often take solace in history: Over the long haul, the U.S. stock market has risen more than it has declined, reflecting the fact that the economy and business activity have expanded and overcome periodic downturns.

Q: What is cost basis?

A: Cost basis can be very important when evaluating your investment. In the simplest terms, your cost basis is how much you paid for an investment. It is an important number to know because it determines your taxable gain or loss when you sell that investment. For example, if you paid $1,000 for 50 shares of a security, your cost basis would be $20 per share. If you were to sell the 50 shares a year later at $25 per share, you'd have a capital gain of $250 ($1,250 - $1,000 = $250). You must report this $250 to the IRS, and pay capital gains tax on it. Not keeping track of your cost basis could cause trouble that can be easily avoided.

Q: I heard about QQQ. What is this and should I invest in it?

A: The QQQ is the index of the NASDAQ. The NASDAQ is the largest electronic trading market in the United States. Generally, these are more aggressive stocks. Anytime you invest more aggressively you are taking on more risk but you also could possibly have greater growth potential. I would wait before you invest in the QQQ. It is like hanging up a valance without first hanging the blinds. You first want to make sure you have your money diversified in small, medium, and large companies as well as internationally before you invest in a specific area or sector. (A **sector** is a specific area of the market or industry group; you could invest in, for example, such as financials, technology types of investments or health care. Investing in a certain kind of **asset class** could be having money invested internationally or in large companies – it's broader than a specific industry.)

BONDS

Q: What is the difference between a stock and a bond?

A: A key difference between a stock and a bond is that stocks make no promises about dividends or returns. A company's dividend may come regularly, but the company is under no obligation to pay it. And while the company stock might be very profitable at one time, it could also go down and cause a loss unexpectedly. When a company issues a bond, however, the company guarantees to pay back your principal (the face value, i.e., what you paid to buy it) plus interest. If you buy the bond and hold it to maturity, in most cases you know exactly how much you are going to get back; this is why bonds are also known as "fixed-income" investments. Be aware, though, that the guarantee from the company is only as good as the company's ability to pay you back. If the company is no longer around and they have gone bankrupt, the likelihood of getting your money back is low; just because a bond is considered fixed income does not necessarily mean it is a safe investment.

Q: What is a corporate bond?

A: A corporate bond is a bond issued by a corporation to raise capital, i.e., money for the corporation. Basically, you are loaning the company money in exchange for interest payments. The principal value of bonds – the amount of money you loaned them – may fluctuate due to market conditions. If redeemed before maturity – the date on which you will get your money back, plus the interest you have earned – bonds may be worth more or less than the original investment.

Q: Are there different kinds of corporate bonds?

A: Corporate bonds come in dozens of varieties. Many feature a

call provision that allows the issuing company to pay back the principal to bond holders before maturity. Other corporate bonds are known as **convertibles** because they carry a provision that the bond can be converted into shares of common stock under certain circumstances. Convertible bonds can be more attractive than bonds with no conversion provision, depending on the price of the underlying stock. Most corporate bonds are **fixed-rate** bonds. The interest rate the corporation pays is "fixed" until maturity, which means it will never change.

Q: How can I be sure the company is a good bet for bonds?

A: Rather than take the company's word for it, you can check with companies that specialize in evaluating corporations and other bond issuers to determine their financial strength. Best, Moody's, Fitch, and Standard & Poor's rating services all specialize in assigning ratings to bonds that determine the ability of their issuers to repay those bonds. Make sure you know the conditions and specifics of the corporate bond and do your research about the bond through outside resources.

Q: What is a municipal bond?

A: A municipal bond is issued by a state, municipality, or county, in order to finance its capital expenditures. Basically, you are loaning the government money to build things like a new school, roads or buildings. Municipal, or "muni," bonds are exempt from federal taxes and from most state and local taxes, especially if you live in the state where the bond is issued; alternative minimum tax may apply, though. (Minnesota residents who buy Minnesota municipal bonds will not pay Minnesota state taxes or federal taxes. However, if you purchase a municipal bond from another state, you will pay state taxes on the municipal bond.) Know and understand the tax implications on the municipal bond and research the bond to make sure it is a good investment. Muni bonds are subject to availability and change in price; they are also subject to market and interest-rate risk if you sell the bond before maturity. Also, bond values will decline as interest rates rise. Interest income may be subject to the alternative minimum tax.

Q: What are Series EE bonds?
A: Series EE bonds are U.S. savings bonds. They replaced the old series E bonds in 1980. Savings bonds are safer, low-risk investments. You buy a bond and it will mature in thirty years. These bonds will no longer carry variable interest rates; newly purchased bonds will carry fixed rates for at least twenty years. Bonds are no longer issued that mature in 30 years.

Q: How will the fixed interest rate affect the series EE bond?
A: The savings bonds no longer have a floating interest rate and will now have a fixed interest rate. Depending on whether there is a rise or decline in rates the fixed rate may benefit your investments. For example: a family buys one $100 EE bond a month from the time their child turns five until the child turns eighteen. With a fixed rate of 3.25 percent, each bond would be worth $19,380.93 after thirteen years. If the rate had not been fixed, and assuming interest rates rise so the average annual yield is 4.5 percent, the bonds would be worth $21,147.42 after thirteen years. If interest rates are declining, that would reduce the average annual yield to 2 percent, and the bond would be worth $17,798.97.

INVESTING STRATEGY

Q: What is asset allocation?
A: If you are one of the many Americans who believe your best investment strategy is to buy low and sell high, you may want to explore the merits of asset allocation. Studies of some of America's major pension funds have shown that an asset allocation policy is the major element that determines

how the portfolio performs. Although no investment strategy can guarantee success, a properly allocated portfolio (one that is well diversified) is more likely to do well as the markets do well, and offer some stability if markets aren't doing well. It is important to rebalance your portfolio periodically and to watch your allocation so that you are not overexposed in a certain area – that is, you have too many eggs in one basket – or that your portfolio is more aggressive (or taking on more risk) than you want it to be without knowing it. When I talk about asset allocation, I describe five boxes and a big circle. The big circle is the fixed-income category, which is made up of CDs, money market accounts, and bonds, which are your "safer" types of investments. The five boxes are "growth" investments, which consist of large-cap growth, large-cap value, mid-cap, small-cap, and international. These are different types of investments, and that's the point: It's important to have your money diversified.

Money Tip:

If you don't understand an investment don't buy it.

- **Large-cap:** Anytime you hear the word "cap" it means "capital," which refers to the size of the company. Large cap are huge, blue-chip corporations. These are the big corporations that are often household names. Within these areas there is growth and value

- **Growth and value:** Growth is buying into companies that have great growth potential. The stocks may not be inexpensive but they could be well worth it, particularly because these are companies that could have the potential to grow at a faster rate than other companies. Value is buying into companies that are a great value or at a discount.

If you are a coupon clipper or look to buy things when they are on sale, that's an example of looking for that good value. With a company, "value" usually means the price per share has gone down from its previous stock price. So the stock could be at a discount – hence the value. Be careful, though: Some stocks that go down just keep going down so value is not just measured a low stock price. The company needs to be a great company and undervalued.

- **Small- and mid-cap:** You also want to have money in small and medium-sized companies. These are companies that could be more aggressive, but generally not all companies' share prices go up at the same time. Most of the time not all areas of the market are doing well at the same time and by owning a bunch of different-size companies you keep your portfolio diversified.

- **International:** It's also important to have your dollars invested internationally, that is, in companies based outside the United States. We now live in a global economy, so investing internationally is another way to help diversify. Be aware, however, that international investing involves special risks including country, currency, and geo-political risk, as well as increased volatility of foreign securities and differences in accounting practices, currency fluctuation and political instability, and may not be suitable for all investors.

Q: How does asset allocation help my investments?

A: Asset allocation is the process of spreading your money across stocks, bonds, and cash equivalents in a way that reflects your goals and risk tolerance. Allocation is the primary driver of your investment performance – how well your investments do. The appropriate asset allocation strategy can help reduce the risk associated with any one investment and potentially enhance returns. A number of factors go into choosing an asset allocation that addresses your particular goals and situation, which can include but are not limited to: your "investment horizon," which is how much time you have to invest; your risk tolerance, which is how well you can handle the volatility of the stock market; and your overall financial profile. Your allocation also depends a lot on how much money you have, how much you need to have in retirement, and at what age you want to retire, among other factors. Enlisting the aid of a financial advisor can be very helpful as you develop an asset allocation strategy that can work for you. A financial advisor whom you like, and who understands your goals and your dreams can be a great help in creating an asset allocation strategy that is right for you.

Q: I am wondering how I can make more on my investments. I have about $420,000, with 10 percent in cash, about 30 percent in bonds, and 60 percent in stocks. Is this a good allocation?

A: How much money you should have in stocks or bonds in your portfolio will depend on your individual situation and financial goals. As your circumstances change over time, your financial advisor can adjust the weightings in your portfolio to reflect your goals. For example, in your earlier investment years, you will probably want a larger portion of your assets invested in stocks for long-term growth. Although past performance cannot guarantee future results, equities (otherwise known as stocks) have historically outperformed other investment classes. As you approach retirement age, you may want to shift more of your assets into less volatile investments, such as fixed income instruments like bonds, CDs, or money market accounts.

Q: I make about $75,000 a year and am maxing out my 401(k) and my IRAs. I have two kids, and feel like I am paying too much in taxes on my taxable accounts. Any suggestions?

A: While it is virtually impossible for investors to avoid taxes, there are several strategies you can use to reduce or defer taxes. These common-sense strategies can reduce the tax burden of your taxable investment portfolios. For example, even the best stock portfolios are likely to have a few holdings that are not meeting your expectations. Selling a stock at a loss can make sense if it can be replaced with another holding that offers an attractive return. A stock that you sold to take a loss means that you realized that loss – you sold the stock to take advantage of the loss. (Until you actually sell the stock, no matter what it says on paper, you really haven't lost anything). The realized capital loss can be used to offset capital gains that are realized for the same year (that is, money you made by selling stocks). Losses also can be carried forward over to the next several tax years, if necessary; you want to work with your accountant on this. You could also look at donating money to charity, making sure you are taking advantage of the deductibility of interest on your mortgage and analyzing your investments to see if you can have some more tax-efficient investments.

RETURNS ON INVESTMENT

Q: What is the Rule of 72?

A: The rule of 72 is a simple formula that helps you quickly approximate a possible investment goal given a particular rate of return. If you divide 72 by the interest rate that you hope to earn on an investment, you will have an estimate of how many years it could take for your money to double. For example, over the last seventy years the stock market has produced an average return of 11.1 percent. If you round that down to 10 percent and plug it into the formula, you find that your money could hypothetically double every 7.2 years. Investments are subject to market fluctuation so there is no assurance that any investment will double in value. The rule of 72 is a mathematical concept and does not guarantee investment results or function as a predictor of how an investment will perform. It is simply an approximation of the impact a targeted rate of return would have. Investments are subject to the fluctuating returns and there is no assurance that any investment will double in value.

Q: How much should I be earning on my investments?

A: Most financial advisors generally advise a goal of earning, on average, 8 to 10 percent on average over the years – but as always, it depends on your age, how much you have saved so far, and your goals. If you don't need or want to take on a lot of risk you could invest in fixed-income securities where you could earn 6 percent; on the other hand, if you have a higher risk tolerance you could invest in the stock market where one year you could lose 18 percent but the next you could gain 21 percent.

Q: How can I make sure there's enough growth in my investment portfolio?

A: From 1984 to 2002, the Standard & Poor's 500 Index returned 13 percent annually, but the average equity fund investor realized a gain of only 3.5 percent. The difference in returns is primarily because individuals are emotional investors who tend to buy high when the market is hot and sell low when prices fall. That's why it's important to build a investment strategy that can help you stay invested and maximize growth potential in any market. Having a financial advisor can help you create this strategy.

CALLING IN THE PROFESSIONALS

Q: What's the difference between a financial advisor, stock broker, financial planner, investment executive, investment counselor, and the many other titles I run across in the financial world?

A: There are so many different titles, it can definitely be confusing. When you're interviewing someone to help you with your money, first decide what you are looking for. Do you need budgeting help? If so, seek a financial advisor, counselor or planner. Do you need investing help? You could seek out any of the titles above, but you definitely find someone who has a series 7 license. This is the license that allows financial advisors to buy and sell securities. If you want someone to help you with your overall planning, you'll likely want a financial advisor or a financial planner. These titles are confusing for consumers because someone who buys stocks could have any of these, but different advisors may specialize in certain areas. I am a financial advisor and I buy stocks, bonds, and other investments for my clients but it's just as important for me to help my clients with their overall plan and overall situation.

> **Money Tip:**
>
> **I**f you don't have a financial advisor – start interviewing.

Q: A friend recently told me I should hire a money manager. What exactly is a money manager and when should I consider hiring one?

A: A money manager runs your money, along with money from institutions (like, for example, a college or university) and foundations. When you have your money with a money manager, you actually own the individual stocks that they manage in the portfolio. Most money managers, through a financial advisor, require an initial minimum amount of $100,000 to invest. If you have assets of $300,000 or more, you should consider separately managed accounts. In a separately managed account, individual money managers focus on a certain asset class. Money managers have investment policy statements about where the money is invested and are held to strict standards. For example: You have $100,000 with one money manager, who only manages large-cap investments. Again, you would actually own the individual stocks. Then the second $100,000 could be invested in small and medium-sized companies with a separate money manager who specializes in that area; and so on. The important thing is to ask questions so you know how your money is being managed; there's never a dumb question when it comes to your money.

Q: How do financial advisors get paid?

A: Financial advisors typically get paid three main ways: fee-based, commission-based, or hourly.

- In **fee-based accounts**, you pay a certain percentage of your assets that the financial advisor manages. You *don't* pay per transaction – as you do when you buy or sell stock – but pay a set percentage based on the value of your account. Fees typically range from 0.7 to 3 percent industry wide, depending on the size of your accounts. An example of a fee-based account: You have $100,000, and you pay 2 percent for the account; that means you'd pay $2,000 for the year. The fee generally is taken out of your account quarterly, and is the only fee you pay. Please note that in fee-based accounts nominal transactions may apply.
- In **commission-based accounts**, you pay every time you buy and/or sell an investment. This is also known as transaction-based.
- **Hourly** is a straight hourly rate.

One type is not necessarily better than the other. It depends on your situation, how much money you have and how transparent you want your fees to be.

Q: What kind of fees can I expect to pay if I have an account with an investment firm?

A: Wherever your money is, someone is making money off of it; it's always important to look at your statements so you know how much you are paying. Most firms across the financial industry have increased, or are increasing, their account fees. Most firms have an IRA maintenance fee that ranges from $30 to $75 a year, which goes to the IRA custodian (generally the investment firm). We, as financial advisors, don't get a portion of this IRA fee – in fact, we even pay IRA maintenance fees on our own IRA accounts. IRAs (and 401(k)s) are non-taxable accounts – that is, you don't have to pay taxes every year on the earnings in the account. However, some firms are charging account fees on taxable accounts, ranging from $20 to $75 a year. Taxable accounts are accounts where you pay taxes on what you earn every year. They are just like a savings account; they're in your name (or in your name and a spouse's name if it's a joint account); but instead of just having the money sit there and build up interest, you use the money for a variety of investments. So, for example, if you used the money to buy and sell stocks, you'd pay taxes on any money you earn either from interest, dividends, or from capital gains (any profit you might have made from selling a stock). Some firms are even charging small-account fees – that is, if you have less than a certain stated amount in an account they charge you a fee (around $15 to $20 a quarter) just to have the account at their firm.

Q: How does a person find or pick a financial advisor?

A: Start by asking for referrals from friends, family or neighbors; another good way to start is find someone who's financially successful and prepared, and ask them who they use. You can also find financial advisors through community education programs or in local newspaper calendars, which often list seminars. These seminars are a good idea when you're looking for a financial advisor: They help you learn more about money, and they also let you to see the financial advisor in action to get an idea of their style and philosophy. Next, meet with a few advisors individually. Most financial advisors offer a free initial consultation so you can get their opinion on your specific situation and see if there is any chemistry. I encourage you to find someone that you truly trust and feel that you can connect with – it's your money and no one cares more about it than you. And always ask questions so you feel that this person is on the same page with you; there is never a dumb question when it comes to your money.

Q: Why do I want an independent financial advisor?

A: Having an independent financial advisor means they do not have specific investments or certain products they want to sell to you – they can give you truly unbiased advice. They can help you invest in whatever the best investments are for you regardless of the company.

Q: How do I know I can trust the person I invest with?

A: First, ask the advisor if they are licensed and registered in your state. You also want the advisor to give you written information that fully explains the investment you are considering, such as prospectuses. Yes, I know your eyes glaze over when you see a prospectus, which is another reason you need a financial advisor whom you like and can explain things in a way you understand. Next, ask yourself if the claims they are making are realistic; if it looks too good to be true, it usually is. Do your homework; a little research on any returns claimed will help prevent investing in a scam. If they are licensed, you can also look up the financial advisor's record with FINRA (www.finra.org). FINRA is the regulatory body of financial services firms. Finally, always ask yourself if the investment meets your personal investment goals.

Q: I had a financial advisor who worked for a company, then left that firm. Should I follow the financial advisor or stay with the firm?

A: You need to look at why your financial advisor left the firm and analyze your relationship. He or she might have retired, or isn't a financial advisor anymore. If your financial advisor switches companies, whatever you do, don't let someone else make the decision for you. If you have a relationship of trust and confidence, you might want to consider following him or her. I switched firms and clients followed me; I left my prior firm to go independent because I did not want to represent any product or have any bias. If this is why your financial advisor left, and you like them and the service they have given you, I see no reason not to follow him or her.

Q: Do I really need a financial advisor or can I do this on my own?
A: Theoretically yes, but remember: A financial advisor can take your emotions out of your financial decisions, as well as keep up with the tax laws and changes in IRAs, investments, the market, and all the other details. Think about recent history. From March 2000 through December 2001, American households lost more than $5 trillion, or 18 percent of their financial wealth. Many retirees were forced to go back to work or reduce their standard of living. Can you afford to lose your retirement assets in another market downturn? Having a financial advisor can help you protect your assets and help create an investing strategy for your goals.

Q: Every month I receive about eleven financial statements in the mail. Is there a way to put all of my accounts in one place?
A: Yes. If you have multiple accounts at multiple firms, consider consolidating your assets with one firm. Being diversified means not having all your eggs in one basket; it does not mean having accounts with several different brokerage firms. You can have one firm, and within your accounts still have a diversified approach. It also usually helps simplify your life. Some potential advantages a consolidated approach offers:

1. It's easier to allocate, diversify, and rebalance in one portfolio.
2. You'll potentially have lower fees.
3. You'll have one financial advisor to help you with your plan.

4. You can view your accounts online, in one place.

And... you'll get one consolidated statement, not several to fill your mailbox.

Q: What is an investment club?

A: An investment club is a group of people who get together on a regular basis to discuss investments. Everyone pools their money to buy securities; the monthly contribution typically ranges from $25 to $250 a month. Members take turns researching and presenting on companies whose stocks they may be interested in owning. Then the group votes on which stocks to own and use their money together to buy the stock. Once an investment is purchased a member continues to follow the investment and reports at the monthly meeting with any updates.

Q: How do you start an investment club?

A: You can either look to join a club that already exists or find other people who are interested in forming a group. In the second case, you first need to decide how many members you want and any rules for the group, then write a set of bylaws; you are setting up a legal entity. You will then form a legal partnership and can start meeting and collecting money to invest. You can go to www.naic.org for more information about setting up an investment club, or talk to a financial advisor.

CHAPTER 3

RETIREMENT

For most of us, retirement is usually what we're saving the most money for. But it means something different for each one of us. You may want to travel the world, while your spouse may want to stay at home and relax. These are two different ideas and dreams, and they have different monetary needs. In the following chapter, you'll find information about the various types of accounts and options, as well as some of the common questions about retirement.

WHERE DO I START?

Q: There are so many things to think about when it comes to investing that I feel overwhelmed, especially when I think of retirement. Where should I start?

A: You're not alone. Many of us worry about inflation, Social Security, health care costs, retirement income, and the possibility of running out of money. But you can manage – even master – your fears. First, have a plan for the future. Know what you want to do when you retire and where you want to live. If you want to travel a lot, that may cost a lot more than downsizing your house and staying close to home. Once you have a well-defined goal, you'll have something you can work towards achieving. Next, stop comparing yourself to co-workers, family, and friends. Everyone's situation is unique. When you compare yourself to other people, you aren't focusing on what you need and what you have to work with. Don't forget to talk and think about money; trying to forget about it not only won't get rid of the fear, but by tidying up your finances now and making a plan for the future, you'll worry a lot less about your finances and you can put your time and energy toward more important things, like the fun you'll have in retirement spending time with your family!

Q: How do I know if I'm saving enough for retirement?

A: A general recommendation says that men should be saving 10 percent of their income, women 12 percent. However, it's especially important for all of us to actually sit down and develop a plan to figure out if we're are saving enough. Go to a financial website such as www.helpingyouinvest.com and use the financial calculators, or sit down with a financial advisor, who can help you figure out if you're saving enough. Then when the question "Are you saving enough?" comes up, you can say "Yes!"

Q: I think I need to save more money for retirement. Is there a minimum amount I need to start with?

A: Saving for retirement does not have to be "all or nothing." You don't need to make a choice between current financial obligations and saving for retirement – saving a little bit now will have the benefit of the amount of time the money has to grow. A good way to start is to put 1 percent of your paycheck into your 401(k) plan. Most of the time you won't even notice the money coming out of your paycheck; then gradually increase the percentage you contribute.

Q: How do I know if I have enough saved for retirement?

A: It truly depends on who you are and how you answer these three questions:
1) What kind of life do you want in retirement?
2) At what age do you want to retire?
3) How much income do you want in retirement?

For example, if you had $1 million and you locked up that money in a 5 percent fixed-income investment option such as a CD, you could earn $50,000 a year and not even touch your $1 million dollars (your "principal"). That gives you security. But you may decide you want more than that to do the things you'd like. Once you answer these three questions, a financial advisor can help you plan for your retirement, including more specific amounts that you need to save each month to meet your retirement goals.

Q: I'm now fifty-eight. Is it too late for me to save for retirement?

A: It's never too late to start saving for retirement (or any financial goal you may have). The hardest part is starting. First, see if you have a retirement plan where you work; that's the account you should take advantage of first. Just sign up with a small percentage – you probably won't even notice the money being taken out of your paycheck. Then increase the contributions as you feel comfortable. I also would start doing some retirement planning where you can learn specifically how much you need to save every month to reach your retirement goal.

Q: What is a catch-up contribution?

A: If you are more than fifty years old you can make a "catch-up" contribution of $1,000 every year to your IRAs. With 401(k) plans, which you get through your employer, you're allowed to contribute an extra $5,000 every year if you're over fifty.

Q: How can my retirement assets help lower my income tax?

A: The federal income tax rate for a married couple filing jointly ranges from 10 percent to 35 percent depending on your taxable income. If you're married and have taxable income of $150,000 per year, you could give away as much as $31,958 to Uncle Sam. Multiply that figure by forty – the number of years you're likely to be working – and that comes to nearly $1.3 million; that's a lot of money. You can lower your taxes by contributing the most you can to your 401(k) because the dollars that you invest in these accounts are pre-tax; that lowers your income so you pay less in taxes; so, for example, if you make $150,000 and you put $15,000 into your 401(k) plan, you'll pay income taxes on $135,000 ($150,000 - $15,000 = $135,000). Make sure you're taking advantage of these kinds of retirement savings, as well as donations and the other options, to lower your tax bill. No one wants to pay more taxes than they need to.

TYPES OF RETIREMENT ACCOUNTS

INDIVIDUAL RETIREMENT ACCOUNTS (IRAs)

Q: What is an IRA?

A: An IRA stands for individual retirement account. In an IRA you can invest in anything: stocks, bonds, CDs, real estate, and much more. You can be as aggressive or as conservative as you want with your IRA, but there is no set rate of return. An IRA may be in one person's name only. There are two kinds of IRAs, **Traditional** and **Roth**. In the Traditional IRA, there are no income limits; the Roth has some income limits. With a Traditional IRA, you pay income taxes when you take out money in your retirement, at the tax bracket you're in when you retire; with a Roth IRA you don't pay any money on the dollars when you take the money out in your retirement, because you've already paid taxes on those dollars.

Q: When is the deadline to contribute to my IRA?

A: You have until April 15th of the current year to put money away for the previous year in a Roth or Traditional IRA.

Q: What is so important about the age of 59½?

A: That's when you can take money out of your Traditional IRAs without paying the 10 percent penalty. Any money that you do take out of the Traditional IRAs, though, will be subject to state and federal income taxes. There are a few specific ways and certain circumstances under which you can take money out of your IRAs before 59½ without this penalty. I'll discuss those later in this chapter.

Q: Is it true that I have to take money out of my Traditional IRAs when I turn 70½?

A: Yes, the magic age of 70½ is when you are forced to take distributions from your Traditional IRAs. If you don't take your required minimum distributions (RMD) the penalty can be up to 50 percent of the dollar amount you should have withdrawn. This is one more reason to consolidate your accounts so you can take correct distributions when necessary.

Q: I have an enterprising daughter who has earned income through an after-school job. Can she open an IRA?

A: Yes, of course! When setting up an account for someone under 18, a parent or another guardian must sign the paperwork, accepting legal responsibility for investing the child's money. Once established, you and/or the child can contribute an amount equal to his or her income or $5,000, whichever is less. Opening an IRA for your daughter now is a great idea because it not only encourages her to save more, you can also help her choose from a wide range of investment options and track their progress over time. Withdrawals prior to age 59½ are subject to a 10 percent IRS penalty.

Q: I have six different IRAs. Is this OK or should I be doing something different?

A: Many of us think having money in different IRAs with different investment firms is being diversified. It isn't. You want to consolidate these accounts by taking all of them and putting them into one IRA. Why should you do this? First off, you are going to eliminate the clutter from your mailbox. More important, you'll have one financial advisor looking at the big picture instead of just a narrow slice of your finances, and making sure your money is being invested and managed correctly. Lastly, if you have many different IRAs it makes it almost impossible to make sure you have the right distribution dollar amount when you have to start taking distributions at 70½.

Q: I pay an IRA maintenance fee. What is this for?
A: An IRA maintenance fee is for the costs of being a custodian for an IRA and the reporting to the IRS. Generally these fees range from $30 to $75 per IRA per year.

Q: If I max out my Traditional IRA does that prohibit me from adding to my SIMPLE IRA at work?
A: No. In any given year you can add to the Roth or Traditional IRA in addition to the retirement plan you have where you work. At work you can have a 401(k), 403(b), 457 plan, SEP IRA, SIMPLE IRA, pension plan (to name only a few possibilities). Having a SIMPLE IRA is generally for smaller companies that have 100 employees or fewer.

Money Tip:

If you qualify for a Roth IRA – do it!

ROTH IRAs

Q: What is the Roth IRA?
A: The Roth IRA is an option for anyone who earns less than $99,000 or married couples who earn less than $156,000. (I'll discuss options for people over these income limits later in this section.) If you fall within the income limits you can put away $5,000 a year in the Roth IRA; if you are over fifty you can put $6,000 away. If you are a married couple both under the age of fifty you can contribute $10,000 total. If you're a married couple both over fifty, together you can put away $12,000. Generally, the younger you are the more a Roth IRA benefits you. In a Roth IRA you can invest in stocks, bonds, or other investments (one exception: you can't invest in certain collectibles). There

is no set rate of return in a Roth IRA; that is determined by how you invest the money. The Roth IRA does not give you a tax benefit today because the money you put into the account is after-tax dollars. But that means when you go to withdraw in retirement it's tax-free. Withdrawals before age 59½ are subject to a 10 percent IRS penalty.

Q: How do I decide whether to do the Roth or Traditional IRA?

A: There are many things to consider when choosing a Traditional or Roth IRA account. One thing that will make a difference is your current tax bracket. For example, if you are currently in a high tax bracket and expect to be in a much lower tax bracket during retirement, a Traditional IRA could be the best option because you may be able to claim a deduction on your contributions now, then pay taxes on future distributions at the lower rate later. If you can fund a Roth IRA for at least 12 to 15 years before retirement, some experts say you could still come out ahead. Most people who meet the income limits choose the Roth IRA because you don't pay a single cent of tax on any money you earn in the Roth IRA.

Q: Do you have to take money out of the Roth IRA when you turn 70½?

A: No. One of the key advantages of the Roth IRA is that it does not require the account owner to take distributions during his or her lifetime. In addition, you can continue to make contributions to a Roth IRA beyond age 70½ as long as you have earned income. Another major benefit of the Roth IRA is that distributions taken by the owner, or the owner's beneficiaries, are generally tax-free if the owner has held the account for at least five years and meets certain other requirements. The Roth IRA is a great vehicle to take advantage of if you meet the income limit requirements.

Q: I was told there are income limitations on the Roth IRA. What are they?

A: If you make less than $99,000 as a single person, you can put away

$5,000 a year, $6,000 if you're over 50. A single person making between $99,000 and $114,000 may put away some money in the Roth IRA. Once you make more than $114,000 you cannot add to a Roth IRA. If you're a married couple both under fifty with an income of under $156,000, together you may put away $10,000 total; if you're both over fifty, that limit rises to $12,000. If you as a couple make between $156,000 and $166,000 you may put some money in the Roth IRA. Once the two of you make more than $166,000 you cannot contribute to the Roth IRA at all. In both the single and married cases, though, you can still have a Roth IRA, you just can't add to it. Also be aware that the income limits could change from year to year.

Q: I am single, forty-seven and made $187,000 last year at my job. I contributed to my Roth for last year but I think I cannot contribute because of my income. Is this true? If so, what do I do?

A: You're right; you can't contribute because you're over the income limits. You need to take the dollars that you put into the Roth IRA and "recharacterize" the contribution to a Traditional IRA. This is paperwork that your financial advisor can help you complete.

Q: My income has been significantly lower this past year, putting me in the lowest tax bracket. I expect the situation to improve so that I'll soon be in a higher tax bracket. Would now be a good time to switch my Traditional IRA to a Roth IRA?

A: It might be. In any given year anyone who earns income within certain income limits is allowed to put away $5,000 ($6,000 if you're over fifty) per year into the Roth IRA or Traditional IRA. You could also make a contribution *and* do a Roth IRA conversion.

Q: What is a Roth conversion?

A: A Roth conversion is when you take money that's in a Traditional IRA and put these dollars in a Roth IRA. You can even do a conversion on money that is from an old 401(k) plan. Let's say you worked at a company and had $8,000 in your retirement plan, then you left the company. Any time you leave a company you may want to take that money and roll it into a Traditional IRA. Once the money is in the Traditional IRA you can do a Roth conversion. That means you take that $8,000, pay income taxes on the money today, then invest those dollars within the Roth IRA. When you do this you are taking pre-tax money and making it after-tax, so this is a "taxable event" for which you'll pay state and federal income taxes on the dollar amount you convert. However, when you take the money out of the Roth in retirement you will not pay taxes. A Roth conversion may benefit you in your retirement and is something you can discuss with your financial advisor.

Note: **A conversion is different from a contribution**. You can do a Roth conversion of that $8,000 and you can also make your annual contribution of $5,000 if you are under 50 ($6,000 if you are over fifty) in the same year you do a conversion, as long as you qualify.

Q: I am just starting to participate in the retirement plan offered through my employer and would like to save even more for retirement. Where should I start?

A: The Roth IRA is a great vehicle. If you don't qualify to contribute to the Roth IRA, you could add to a Traditional IRA without the deduction (which you can get on the Traditional IRA if your income is low enough). Beyond your retirement plan at work and the IRA you can open a taxable account in your own name (or in your name and your spouse's if it's a joint account). This is a regular account where you have money invested – it could be in CDs, bonds, stocks, etc., but you have to pay taxes each year on whatever you earn.

Q: Can I open up a Roth IRA for my daughter to use for college education expenses? She is fourteen and I already am doing the Coverdell account. If I can open a Roth for her, how do I do it?

A: If your daughter is working and has earned income, yes, you can open a Roth IRA for her. The money in a Roth IRA can be used for higher education, a first home purchase or for her own retirement later on, but she can only contribute as much as she has earned each year. So if your daughter makes $1,000 in the summer she can put $1,000 into the Roth IRA; however, if you like, you could make the $1,000 contribution for her.

Q: My Roth IRA is losing money. Should I take the money out and put it in a savings account?

A: Absolutely not. When you put money in a Roth IRA you can invest in almost anything, so it's not that the Roth IRA is the wrong vehicle for you, it's how you have the money invested in it. Besides, if you take the money out of the Roth and put it into a savings account, you could pay a penalty.

Q: My husband works full time and makes about $80,000 a year. I'm a stay-at-home mom. Can I do the Roth IRA?

A: Yes. You don't have to work to have a Roth IRA. The main requirement for the Roth IRA is to have earned income or be married to someone who has earned income, as long as you file a joint return with your spouse.

Q: I would like to start investing in a Roth IRA, but all the ones I've researched require a large initial contribution. Is there a Roth available that can be opened for less than $1,000? I plan on contributing to it on a regular basis after that.

A: Generally, you should be able to set up a Roth IRA without making an initial lump-sum contribution but instead contributing every month automatically. Some firms do have minimum investment amounts but most of these are set by the investment company that sells the product you're investing in. Most financial advisors can help you with a Roth IRA with no contribution and set it up for your automatic contribution every month. You want one IRA where you add to every year; inside of that one IRA is where you can invest in stocks, bonds or other investment vehicles.

STRETCH IRAS

Q: What is a Stretch IRA?

A: How many people do you know who have inherited money and blown it all within a few months (or maybe even a few days)? If you plan properly a Stretch IRA can provide a lifetime of income for the owner or the beneficiaries. This kind of IRA allows you to control how your beneficiaries receive money after your death, and it's one of the best gifts you can give. I believe it's much better for someone to receive $1,000 a month for the rest of their life instead of a few hundred thousand dollars at one time that tempts them to foolishly spend and have little or nothing to show for it. On top of that, the heirs of your IRA won't have to deal with avoidable income- and estate-tax issues.

RETIREMENT PLANS WHERE YOU WORK

401(K)S

Q: What is a 401(k) plan?

A: A 401(k) plan is a retirement plan offered by your employer that allows you to put away money that you don't have to pay taxes on every year. You may put away up to $15,500 each year if you are under fifty, $20,500 if you're over fifty. Your employer-sponsored retirement plan (which is your 401(k), 403(b) or 457 plan – it depends on where you work) is one of your most valuable assets. Qualified retirement plans remain one of the most significant tax and investment benefits available. Review your retirement plan at work and know the answer to the following questions:

- Are you taking full advantage of your plan?

Money Tip:

Max out your 401(k). Especially if you have a match, that's *free* money!

- Does your retirement plan at work offer a match (that is, your employer will match a portion of your contributions with dollars from the company)?
- If so, are you making sure you contribute enough so you get the match?
- How appropriately allocated are your retirement assets?
- Does your retirement plan complement your other investments?

Q: Why is a 401(k) plan so beneficial?

A: 401(k) plans are beneficial for a number of reasons. First, your contributions are deductible right from your paycheck and these are pre-tax dollars. Eventually you will pay tax both on your contributions and on any investment gains in your account, but that does not happen until you withdraw your money at retirement. Another benefit is that in some cases, your employer also matches a portion of whatever you contribute. The match varies from employer to employer so check with your benefits department, but matching 50 percent of the first 6 percent of your contribution is a pretty common arrangement. There is also a Roth 401(k), which is similar to a regular 401(k) but the dollars you put in are after-tax dollars – in other words, you don't pay taxes on what you earn on the money in the Roth 401(k) when you take it at retirement. If your company offers you a match, though, those dollars will still go to your regular 401(k).

Q: How much can I contribute to my 401(k) plan this year?
A: You can put $15,500 a year away in your 401(k). If you are over fifty you can put $20,500 away. This money goes in before taxes so it can actually help you on your taxes, so make sure you're maxing out your retirement plan at work. Maxing out means putting away at least all the money you need so you get a match from your employer (if they offer one). Truly maxing out your 401(k) plan means contributing the total amount allowable.

Q: What does it mean that my company matches 50 percent up to 3 percent on my 401(k)?
A: This means that if you put in 3 percent of what you make in your 401(k) your company will match 50 cents for every dollar up to 3 percent: A match is free money! So if your company offers a match up to X percent, make sure you contribute at least that percentage to get this extra benefit. You can always contribute beyond that percentage if you are able to.

Q: I just started a new job and they offer a 401(k). Should I sign up?
A: Yes, sign up right away! Don't procrastinate because you might forget and would be giving up valuable time and money you could be saving for retirement. When you do sign up, remember to sign up for the maximum percentage possible. You always want to invest enough so you get a match, because that's free money!

Q: Is it better to do my 401(k) where I work, or the Roth IRA?
A: It depends. Ideally you should max out both. The first place to start is to max out your 401(k) plan so you at least get a match (if your employer offers one), then do the Roth IRA. Then come back to the 401(k) plan if you're able to save more. This will allow you to save money pre-tax and post-tax and take the most advantage of any available company match.

Q: My 401(k) has dramatically dropped in value and feels like a "201(k)." What do I do? I have lost a lot of money and this is my only retirement savings. I want to protect my money but I also need it to grow!

A: Have you ever gone and looked at your 401(k) statement and sold holdings that have lost you money to buy last year's winners? (Be honest; lots of people have). This is buying high and selling low – not the right thing to do. Instead, seek out a financial advisor to help rebalance these assets at least once a year. Rebalancing will take the money and reallocate the dollars in different asset classes and therefore could help diversify your 401(k).

Q: I am contributing the max to my 401(k) plan, but I think I'm going to want more money when I retire than this will provide. What else should I be doing for retirement?

A: Good for you for maxing out your 401(k) contributions! Even better, you're already thinking ahead to whether this will be enough when it comes time for your retirement; few of us get started early enough or stick to saving and investing money our entire career. To make up for it, a Traditional or Roth IRA is a good first place to look. Beyond that you could open an account just in your name and contribute after-tax dollars – what's sometimes known as a taxable account. There is no limit on the amount you can invest but you will pay taxes on this account every year on any interest, dividends and possibly capital gains.

Q: I am thinking of buying a house. Should I take a loan against my 401(k) so I can put more down on the house?

A: No, absolutely not. Taking a loan against your 401(k) is the ultimate last resort. You don't want to use assets that are meant to be for your retirement for a house. Instead, you want to build up some liquid money for the down payment. If you don't have enough liquid money you may not be ready to purchase a home yet.

Q: I have a 401(k) plan at work and am able to take a loan. I have some credit card debt that I want to pay off. Should I take a loan on my 401(k) to get rid of this debt?

A: No. Taking a loan against your retirement plan is the last, let me repeat, the LAST resort. I would rather see you use equity in your house or take out a personal loan. If you borrow from your 401(k) plan, then you end up quitting your job or getting laid off, most companies require that you immediately have to pay the loan back. If you don't repay it, you will have to pay the state and federal income tax, and if you are under 59½, you'll also pay a 10 percent penalty on the amount that you took out as a distribution. This amounts to double taxation: 401(k) dollars are pre-tax dollars and if you are let go from the company, you'll be paying back the loan with after-tax dollars.

Q: I'm going into a nursing program full-time for a year. Since I'll be at school, I won't be able to work as I have been. My husband wants to borrow money from his 401(k). I was thinking it would be better to take out a home equity loan. I'm forty, and we have kids. We have no credit card debt, but we need my income. What do you think would be the best way to go about this?

A: Taking a loan against a 401(k), or cashing one in, really is the ultimate last resort. So you can tell your husband that (at least this time), you're right. Depending on your income, student loan interest may be deductible; the interest on a home equity loan is as well. I would look around and compare rates. The likely advantage with the student loan is that you will not have to make payments until you are done with school. You may also want to consider working part time. You have many options, but taking a loan from your 401(k) shouldn't be one of them. Meet with your financial advisor or talk to someone who can advise you on your specific situation.

Q: What does it mean to be vested?

A: If you are 100 percent vested in your company's retirement plan, such as your 401(k), that means if you leave your employer you will receive all the money the company has given you as a match. Some companies have a vesting schedule where you receive a great percentage of the match they have given you. Check your company's vesting schedule so you don't leave your company a few weeks short of being fully vested. Most companies nowadays qualify you as fully vested after working for that employer for five years.

ROTH 401(K)S

Q: What is the Roth 401(k)?

A: The Roth 401(k) may be offered through your employer. It works like the Roth IRA: you can put away money with after-tax dollars, so the money will come out tax-free in retirement. Check to see if one is offered with your benefits package where you work. You can put up to $15,500 in these accounts if you are under fifty years old, $20,500 if you are over fifty. The big difference between a Roth 401(k) and a Roth IRA is that the Roth 401(k) has no income limits.

Q: Should I participate in the Roth 401(k)?

A: It depends. Make sure you have a balance of retirement buckets such as taxable and nontaxable dollars to give yourself the most flexibility. If your employer makes a contribution to your 401(k), those dollars will still go into your regular 401(k); your employer does not contribute to your Roth 401(k). You can contribute to the Roth 401(k) up to $15,500 each year (or $20,500 if over fifty) and there are no income limits with the Roth 401(k). You also want to balance the money that you have in pre-tax – [401(k)] – and post-tax [Roth 401(k)] — accounts. It's a fine balance though, because money you put in the Roth 401(k) will not give you any deduction on your current taxes; on the other hand, you won't pay any taxes on the Roth 401(k) when you take the money out in retirement.

OTHER RETIREMENT ACCOUNTS

Q: Years ago I worked for a company where I had a pension plan. I have not received statements for years. Do I still have money in this plan?

A: With a pension plan, you receive a set amount of money every month once you retire, until you pass away. You might have the option to take this money in a lump-sum, though, which means you could take the pension money and put it immediately in an IRA in your own name when you no longer work at the company. Make sure you look at your pension plans today and be aware of them. Think you're owed a pension from a company you no longer work for? You may be listed among the missing. The Pension Benefit Guaranty Corporation (PBGC), a government agency that stands behind the pension benefits of American workers, is looking for 22,000 people who are owed $80 million from terminated defined-benefit pension plans. To see if you have a missing pension plan, go to www.pbgc.gov. The range of specific benefits owed to each individual is vast. Some are owed as little as $1, others as much as $172,000, pension officials have said. The average benefit owed is about $3,000. If you leave a company and have a pension or a 401(k), it's a good idea to take these accounts and roll them to an IRA in your own name so you have control.

Q: What is an ESOP plan?

A: An ESOP stands for employee stock ownership plan. Generally with an ESOP you can buy stock in the company you work for at a 10, 12, or 15 percent discount compared with the price the general public pays.

Q: How do stock options work?

A: Stock options are not that complicated (although the taxes can be complicated). A stock option is simply the right to buy a stock at a certain price at a point in time. So let's say your employer, ABC Company, gives you 100 stock options at $10. That allows you to buy 100 shares of ABC Company at $10 a share. Then let's say right now ABC Company is trading at $30 a share. That means you can buy 100 shares of ABC company at $10, then immediately turn around and sell them for the current stock price (in our example, $30). You just made $20 on each share of stock. Remember, however, that stock options may expire at a certain date so don't forget to use them before they expire. Where stock options do get more complicated is their tax treatment. Some stock options are considered ordinary income and some are capital gains, depending on whether they are statutory or not.

Q: What does it means when a stock option is statutory?

A: Basically there are two types of stock options: Statutory (qualified) or non-statutory (non-qualified). When statutory stock options are exercised, the profits are taxed as capital gains. When a non-statutory stock option is exercised the profits are taxed as ordinary income.

Q: What is the difference between a 403(b), 457, and a 401(k)?

A: The difference in the simplest form is where you work. If you work as a school teacher, a nurse, or at a non-profit organization you probably have a 403(b) plan. If you work for the federal government you may have a 457. If you work for a publicly or privately held company you may have a 401(k) plan.

ROLLOVERS

Q. I'm leaving my job. What do I do with the money in my employer retirement plan?

A: When you leave an employer you generally have four options for handling the money in your retirement plan.

1. Leave it in your former employer's plan. If your plan balance is less than $5,000, this option is available only if the plan allows it.

2. Transfer your old 401(k) plan to your new employer's plan. Current tax laws make this easier to do, but each plan still has its own rules for what assets it will accept.

3. Take the money as cash. The downside of this option is that you'll pay state and federal income taxes, including a 10 percent penalty tax if you're under age 59½ , and you'll put your future retirement needs at risk.

4. The last option, and what most financial advisors recommend, is to roll over the money into an IRA. Money from a 401(k), 403(b), a profit-sharing plan, money purchase plan, and even a 457 plan can all be invested in a rollover IRA.

Q: What's an IRA rollover?

A: It's when you take money from old 401(k), 403(b) or 457 plans and roll them into a Traditional IRA Rollover. You can do this if you quit your job, are disabled, or because of divorce or death of a spouse.

An IRA Rollover account works just like your 401(k) but is not attached to your employer, and you can invest the money in almost anything: individual stocks, exchange traded funds, CDs, to name a few options. The IRA Rollover can be one account that you can use to consolidate all of your old 401(k), 403(b), and 457 plans.

Q: Why should I roll my old 401(k) into my IRA?

A: If you're like most people, you may not have paid much attention to your investments, other than glancing at the plan's quarterly reports. Now everything is changing – you have control over your money and you need to make an informed decision. By rolling it into a Traditional IRA, you gain control over your money. You have more beneficiary options but more important, you can have a financial advisor to help you invest, manage, and rebalance your accounts. There are no taxes and no penalties as long as you do a direct rollover and don't spend any of the money.

Q: My husband will be leaving his job to start school and we are wondering what's the best thing to do with his 401(k). Should we roll it into a Roth IRA?

A: You actually cannot roll it directly to a Roth IRA because a Roth is after-tax dollars and your 401(k) is pre-tax. You can take the money and do a direct rollover into a Traditional IRA and then do a Roth conversion. When you do this, be aware you will be paying income taxes on all the money you convert, but after that you have the money in a Roth IRA. Generally, the best thing is to roll your old 401(k) into a Traditional IRA; then if you decide that a Roth conversion is the best thing to do, you can. Right now, you can do a Roth conversion as long as your income is less than $100,000 a year. In 2010 you'll be able to do a Roth conversion no matter what your income.

Q: If a person gets an inheritance from a parent's IRA, can that be rolled into my 401(k) without penalty?

A: It would actually be best if the money goes to you as a beneficiary IRA. These dollars are then *transferred* – not distributed – to you, so you don't pay taxes on it. If the money is *distributed* to you from an IRA you will have to pay state and federal income taxes on the money. As a beneficiary IRA, the money is in your name. These dollars can then be withdrawn within five years of the inheritance or based on your life expectancy.

Q: What is the difference between an indirect and a direct rollover?

A: With an **indirect rollover** a check is made out to you rather than to your new IRA custodian. The custodian is the financial institution that is responsible for your account; it's generally where your account is. With an indirect rollover, your employer is required to withhold 20 percent to meet your potential income-tax obligation. You can get the 20 percent back if you complete the rollover within 60 days, but you must deposit the full amount of the distribution in your new IRA, making up the withheld 20 percent out of other resources for the time being. Also keep in mind that the 20 percent withholding is NOT your ultimate tax liability. If you spend the lump-sum distribution rather than reinvest it in another tax-qualified retirement account, you will have to declare the full value of the lump sum as income and pay the full tax at filing time, depending on your eventual tax bracket. In addition, the IRS generally imposes a 10 percent penalty tax on withdrawals taken before age 59½ from an IRA. A **direct rollover** is where your money goes directly from your old 401(k) to your IRA, no money is withheld and you do not have to pay taxes because no money was distributed to you. (It was rolled over to your IRA.)

Q: Over the years I have opened a number of 401(k) plans and IRAs with a number of different firms. Can I move these into one account?

A: Yes. A Rollover IRA may be the best solution for consolidating multiple retirement accounts. It can help streamline portfolio planning while simplifying account management and distribution decisions. Aside from these efficiencies, IRA Rollovers offer a number of additional benefits.

- *Flexibility*. Having a Traditional IRA Rollover allows you a lot more control. Unlike employer-sponsored retirement accounts, Rollover IRAs allow you to make key decisions that affect account management and administrative costs, investment direction, and asset allocation.

- *Investment choice*. An IRA provides the broadest range of investment choices, and you can develop the precise mix of investments that best reflects your personal risk tolerance, investment philosophy, and financial goals.

- *Robust estate planning features*. Rollover IRAs offer useful estate planning features. For instance, IRA assets can generally be divided among multiple beneficiaries, each of whom can make use of planning structures such as the Stretch IRA concept, to extend the benefits of tax-deferred investment compounding over their lifetimes.

Q: I have less than $5,000 in an old 401(k) plan and I left that company. My previous company opened up an IRA account for me. Can they do this?

A: Yes, your former employer now has the legal right to take the money out of your 401(k) if your balance is less than $5,000. Your former employer will send you a letter stating you have thirty days to respond. If you don't respond within thirty days they will send you a check if you have less than $1,000, and if you're under 59½ you will have to pay taxes and a 10 percent penalty on this amount. They will not send you a check if you have more than $1,000 and less than $5,000, but they will automatically open an IRA for you. You don't want this. Any time you leave a company, take your money with you by rolling over your old 401(k) plans into an IRA in your own name so you retain control.

TAKING MONEY OUT OF YOUR RETIREMENT PLAN

Q: I am 70 and have heard that I have to start taking money out of my Traditional IRA in a few months. Is this true?

A: Yes, when you turn 70½ you need to take distributions from your Traditional IRA, SEP IRA, or SIMPLE IRA, and 401(k) if you are no longer employed, whether you need the money or not. The annual payment is called your required minimum distribution and is calculated each year according to IRS guidelines. You can always take more than the minimum. If you take only your required minimum distribution, the remaining part of your account balance can continue growing tax-deferred. This is a good reason to do some retirement planning so that you are using all of your accounts to your benefit. There is a penalty of up to 50 percent for taking an incorrect distribution or not taking one at all.

Q: How much is OK to draw out of my retirement accounts every year?
A: The general recommendation is 3 to 6 percent, but it does depend on your situation, including how much money you have and how much you earn on the account each year. It's important not to withdraw too much every year because you'll deplete your assets too quickly and run out of money.

Q: I want to take money out of my IRA and take early retirement. I will be 60 years old next month. Can I do this?
A: Yes – after the age of 59½ you can take money out of your Traditional IRAs without paying the 10 percent penalty, although any money you do take out of the Traditional IRA will be subject to state and federal income taxes.

Q: Can I take money out before 59½ without the penalty?
A: Yes, but you want to work closely with your financial advisor if you are considering it. To do so, you can initiate a 72(t). In this case, you can get money out of retirement accounts before 59½ without the 10 percent penalty but you still pay state and federal income tax. You are also required to make the same dollar-amount withdrawal every year and cannot stop the

distribution until five years or until you are 59½, whichever is later.

Q: I am fifty-eight and need to take a distribution out of my 401(k) for a family emergency. Do I have options?

A: Yes, although this usually is a last-case resort; your retirement money is meant to be for retirement. See about taking out a loan, or look to savings or any other investment accounts first. Still, there might be a time you need some of that retirement cash to cover today's expenses and you do have options. You could take a loan from your 401(k) or a distribution from an old 401(k) or IRA. If you do take your money – from an IRA, a 401(k), or both – before you reach the age of 59½, though, the IRS considers this a premature distribution. That means in addition to owing any income tax that may be due on the money, you will face a 10 percent penalty as well. And while there are a few hardship withdrawals such as a divorce where you could possibly escape the 10 percent penalty, depending on the family emergency, you still will pay income taxes.

Q: I recently left a job. What happens if I cash in my 401(k)?

A: Don't. Not only will you pay a 10 percent penalty along with state and federal income taxes, but you will also lose out on future growth potential. For most people, it means you'll end up with about 40 percent of what you take out. Let's say you're in the 28 percent federal tax bracket and 6 percent state tax bracket; you have an old 401(k) of $10,000 and you are under 59½. Ten percent – $1,000 – will go to the penalty. Then $3,400 will go to federal and state income taxes, so only $5,600 will actually hit your pocket. Talk to a financial advisor about rolling the money from the old company 401(k) into a Traditional IRA. This way your money can continue to grow and you will not pay any penalties or taxes at that time.

Q: I am not yet 59½ but I am wondering if there is any way to avoid the 10 per-cent penalty for taking money out of my 401(k) plan?

A: If you are fifty-five or older and leave your employer you can withdraw from your 401(k) without penalty. If you take a distribution you still have to pay state and federal income taxes. There would be no taxes and no penalty if you did a direct rollover to a Traditional IRA.

Another option might be a loan. If your employer allows it, you can take a loan of up to 50 percent of the value in your 401(k), but this is a last resort. You also have the option of Substantially Equal Periodic Payments (SEPP), where you must withdraw a certain amount every year until 59½, or five years, whichever is longer. This is a decision you want to make with your financial advisor, depending on how it fits into your retirement plan. You want to make sure you have enough money to continue to meet your retirement needs once you start withdrawing from your retirement accounts.

RETIREMENT AND YOUR FAMILY

Q: Are there differences with men and women when it comes to saving for retirement?

A: Over the years, my financial advising practice has taught me that retirement planning presents some special considerations for women. A variety of factors can affect how much money women need to retire. Women not only outlive men by an average of seven years, we also earn considerably less money during our lifetime because of childbearing and family responsibilities, and at wages that amount to an average of 30 percent less than those men earn. Lower wages mean smaller pensions and Social Security payments. Divorce or legal separation also can complicate women's financial futures. I'd also argue that it costs women more to live – just look at dry cleaning or the cost of a haircut.

Q: I have heard that I am stuck in the "sandwich generation." What does this mean?

A: The sandwich generation is the Baby Boom generation, born between 1946 and 1964. You are caught in a demographic "perfect storm" that has you squeezed between the needs of younger and older generations. As life expectancies increase and couples start families later in life, you, the sandwich generation members, are trying to invest for your children's college education, offer support to aging parents, all while saving for your own retirement. But if you're part of this growing group, take heart. There is still time to put together a workable strategy for balancing these and other conflicting demands on your money and time. Here are a few ideas to get you moving in the right direction.

- Set clear priorities.
- Discuss eldercare issues with your parents before they arise.
- Take a broad-based approach to paying for college. This is utilizing a mixture of cash, financial aid, loans and investments for college. You can also see the college section on this for more information.
- Make retirement your long-term priority.

Q: My parents are living on Social Security, a small pension, and $16,000 left in savings. My mom told me money is really tight and they have started using some credit cards. Is there anything that I can do for them?

A: When it comes to a parent, relative or friend, we really cannot change their behavior about money; they have to want to change for themselves. Your parents need to assess their overall situation and see what their options are; they need a plan. It could be a home sale, and/or getting on a budget, among many other options. I would recommend seeing a financial advisor; you could meet with their financial advisor or use your advisor. And what you can do is make sure you take care of your own financial situation so that this does not happen to you. Nothing is worse that not having enough money and feeling like you're a burden on your adult children.

SOCIAL SECURITY

Q: How do I know how much I am going to get from Social Security?

A: You can request a benefits statement online by going to www.ssa.gov, where you can find out your Social Security benefits at age 62, 65, or 67. But you don't want to rely on Social Security for your retirement. Social Security is a tax and not meant to be a retirement plan.

Q: Is Social Security going to be there for me?

A: Views differ, but I've seen reports that Social Security is forecast to be out of money in 2040. At any rate, Social Security was founded to help get unemployed workers working. It's a tax, it's not a retirement account. Whether you should include Social Security in your retirement planning depends on your age; the younger you are, the less I would rely on it. This is yet one more reason why you want to take retirement planning into your own hands.

Q: What happens if I take Social Security at 62? Is it true I might have to pay taxes on it?

A: Yes, if you take Social Security before your full retirement age and make more than about $13,000 a year you may have to pay income taxes on the Social Security income you received in that year. If you take Social Security at or after you've reached your full retirement age, you do not have to worry about being taxed on your Social Security income.

Credit Cards and Scores · Business Ownership · Protecting your Assets · Kids and Money · Divorce · Identity Theft · Budgeting · Money Coming and Going · Investing 101 · Credit Cards and Scores · Protecting your Assets · Kids and Money · Budgeting · Money Coming and Going · Investing 101 · Credit Cards and Scores · Protecting your Assets · Kids and Money · Divorce · Identity Theft · Budgeting · Money Coming and Going · Investing 101 · Credit Cards and Scores · Protecting your Assets · Kids and Money · Divorce · Identity Theft · Budgeting · Money Coming and Going · Investing 101 · Credit Cards and Scores · Protecting your Assets · Kids and Money · Divorce · Identity Theft · Budgeting · Money Coming and Going · Investing 101 · Credit Cards and Scores · Protecting your Assets · Kids and Money · Divorce · Identity Theft · Budgeting · Money Coming and Going · Investing 101 · Credit Cards and Scores · Protecting your Assets · Kids and Money · Divorce · Identity Theft · Budgeting · Money Coming and Going · Investing 101 · Credit Cards and Scores · Protecting

BUSINESS OWNERSHIP

If you have ever dreamt of starting your own business or you are already a business owner, this chapter is for you. If you are an entrepreneur, you know it – I always knew I would own my own business one day, I just didn't know exactly what it would be. And once you turn entrepreneur, it's hard to turn back. But knowledge is as important as having that burning desire to follow your dream.

In this chapter you'll find just a few of the many questions I commonly hear about business ownership. They'll help get you started. Other questions you may have may be specific to your business, your industry, and your priorities, so be sure to seek out specific advice related to your situation.

GETTING STARTED

Q: What are some things I should know financially as a business owner?

A: It's pretty much endless! To start with, you want to know the ins and outs of cash flow on a daily, monthly, quarterly, and yearly basis. You also want to know about buying assets, what things you should pay for and what costs you should not spend the money on in your business. Take insurance: You could spend a lot of money protecting every asset and almost every aspect of your business, but is this truly cost effective? No, it's not. You could also spend every dollar that you make on marketing, but if you don't get any return for it, it's probably not worth it. I would develop a strong budget for your business and realize that it does take a lot of time and money to get your business off the ground. You also want to have a good accountant, financial advisor, attorney, and banker. All of these individuals can help keep you on track.

Q: Where can I borrow money from to start my business?

A: It can be hard in the beginning when you have no history of owning a business. I would recommend establishing a relationship with a banker. Credit unions can be especially helpful because most of them are smaller organizations and you can develop a strong relationship with the staff. There are also many organizations such as the Small Business Administration (SBA) that have loan programs for businesses. I would meet with your accountant, attorney, banker and financial advisor and develop a strong business plan, because your cash-flow analysis and business plan are the documents that will be important to your banker.

Q: When should I establish a line of credit for my business?

A: When you've built up your business so you have positive cash flow. You basically want to ask for money when you don't need it.

Q: I have some friends who are independent contractors and they have a credit card they use every month for their business. They get free trips from the card. Is this OK to do?

A: Yes, there's nothing wrong with this. I have a small-business credit card, and I charge most things for the business on the card, then pay the balance off in full every single month. A general rule to stick with is not to charge more than 30 to 50 percent of your available credit limit every month as long as you are not paying fees or interest or any extra charges.

Some credit card companies give you miles or points to purchase certain items or even offer cash back. From time to time I go online or call the credit card company to redeem the points I have received, and usually choose the cash-back option.

Q: I am renting space and a lot of my business-owner friends have been purchasing buildings for their office space. Should I do this?

A: It depends. We bought an office building because it was space for us that would be paid off in twenty years, and it was also less expensive to own than rent. However, you must consider whether you have the time (and patience) to manage owning a building and everything that goes along with it, such as making sure the security system works, the grass is mowed, the light bulbs are replaced, etc. – or whether you have the money to pay someone to manage it for you.

Q: What resources are available for me as a business owner?

A: You have many organizations and groups you can go to. To start with, check into local Chambers of Commerce, the Small Business Administration (SBA), local trade organizations and industry groups. There are also resources for specific types of business owners, for example, the National Association of Women Business Owners (NAWBO).

Q: How do I keep track of all of the money for my business?

A: I would use a computer program to keep track of all your money coming in and out. I use Quickbooks for my office and my businesses. You can choose to do things yourself or you can hire a CPA or a bookkeeper to help you do your books. The benefits of taking care of the books yourself is that you stay on top of the numbers and projections of your business, and of course it doesn't cost you anything except your time. You also don't have to worry about someone compromising your financial information. The downside is that it's time-consuming and a learning process to make sure you're using your computer program correctly.

Q: What kind of business entity should I set myself up as?

A: There are many options, including: an S Corporation, C Corporation, Limited Liability Corporation (LLC), and Limited Liability Partnership (LLP). Choosing the right one for you will depend on taxes, personal liability issues and how you want to structure of your organization. The best thing to do is to meet with your attorney and accountant to help determine which option makes the most sense for you, your business and your goals.

Q: How do I track of everything and pay my employees?

A: You want to set up payroll for your employees. You can do this through your CPA or through a payroll provider; Paychex and ADP are two of the nation's better-known providers. If you do it yourself you can save money but it's time-consuming, plus you need to be sure you file taxes correctly and in a timely manner. If you use a service, do your homework and compare several for service and cost.

Q: What can or should I charge for my hourly rate? I am a consultant and have over twenty years of experience.

A: First, find out what the going rate is with someone with about the same level of experience in your area, then consider how you stack up. A long time ago, someone told me that if you're too comfortable stating your hourly rate, you're not charging enough. Women especially tend to undervalue their competence and expertise. According to this piece of advice, keep raising your rate until it feels almost uncomfortable to tell someone.

Q: What do I do about taxes for my business?

A: If you are a corporation you will need to file a separate return, these are due March 15th of every year (not April 15th, when most people think of filing their personal returns). It's usually worth it to have an accountant file your return. Having someone prepare your taxes and give you advice based on your specific situation can allow you to focus on what you do best, which is run your business.

Q: How much should I pay for employees?

A: I would pay based on experience and what the going rate is. You can look at advertisements and placements in your area to see what similar employers offer. And remember, sometimes it's not just the money that will bring in top-notch employees – added benefits can also make a difference. So even if you're struggling to hire that first full-time employee and you can't offer a large salary, maybe you could pay for their health insurance or give them a bonus opportunity or a retirement plan.

Q: I have two part-time employees and am thinking I need to hire someone full time. How can I decide whether this is worth the expense?

A: Things to consider beyond their salary or hourly wage are benefits and insurance, which can dramatically eat into your bottom line. Other costs include payroll taxes, workers compensation insurance, and the cost of the space for your employee. Once you have these factors in place, then you can make a more informed decision; often, business owners find that in spite of the cost, adding employees can help them become more efficient and grow their business faster.

BENEFITS

Q: I'm a new business owner and have two full-time employees. I want to start offering benefits. Where do I start?

A: First you'll want to look into what kind of health, life and disability insurance you could offer that best benefits both you, the business owner, and your employees.

Benefits are expensive, so you want to look at which benefits are important to your employees and which benefits you can start with. I find that most employers start with health insurance, then a retirement plan, then, when they can, they usually set up a life and disability insurance plan. Beyond that, you can consider any bonus plan structure you can set in place, paid time off, health savings accounts, stock purchase plans and the list goes on and on.

Q: Why should I set up a retirement plan for my business?

A: It can help you on your own taxes, it can help you in your own retirement, and many employers are learning it can be a smart business decision. It's hard enough finding good employees these days (we won't even mention the expense of training). Why risk losing them to another employer just because you lack a good retirement plan?

Q: What are my options for starting a retirement plan for my business that can help me as a business owner?

A: Most sole proprietors or business owners start with the SEP IRA. SEP stands for simplified employee pension; it's for self-employed individuals. The SEP IRA is an individual retirement account where you can save up to 25 percent of your net income from the business up to $46,000 a year. The money that you contribute to the SEP IRA is also another deduction for you on your tax return. A SEP IRA is easy and relatively inexpensive to set up, similar to setting up a Roth or Traditional IRA. Your financial advisor can help you set up a SEP IRA. We just need your name, address, phone number, Social Security number, drivers' license and your financial information such as your risk tolerance, net worth, income, and a few other pieces of financial information.

Q: What are some options for setting up retirement plans?

A: Most business owners start with a SEP IRA, which is inexpensive and easy to set up. When the funds are withdrawn from the accounts after 59½ these dollars will be taxed at ordinary income levels for state and federal taxes. Your employees must all receive the same benefits if eligible. Employees are eligible if they:

- Are at least twenty-one years old.
- Have received $500 in wages for the year.
- Have worked for you at least three of the last five years.

If you have goals as a business to grow, and have a number of employees, you may want to look beyond the SEP IRA at your other options, which include but are not necessarily limited to the 401(k), SIMPLE IRA, money purchase plan, and pension plan. You want to meet with a financial advisor and your accountant to help determine which plan makes the most sense for you.

Q: I work full time for a company but have started a business on the side. I contribute to my 401(k) plan and am maxing out my Roth. I have heard you mention the SEP IRA. Is this something I can also contribute to?

A: Yes, every year you can contribute the maximum to a 401(k) plan where you work, to a Roth or a Traditional IRA (depending on which you qualify for), and to a SEP IRA if you have a business on the side. This is a huge advantage for saving for retirement. The SEP IRA is for small-business owners and you can contribute up to 25 percent of your net income from the business up to $46,000, but you need to be making money on your side business for this to work.

Q: I have a 401(k) plan for my company and we never get any help from my 401(k) provider. Am I stuck or can I do something about this?

A: You can look at changing 401(k) providers; there sometimes can be penalties or charges to change your 401(k) plan but if you are paying for a service you're not getting, it may be worth it to switch. As an employer, you don't want to tell your employees how they should invest in their account, but you want them to get help and advice. As a financial advisor who helps companies with their 401(k) plans, I love to hold seminars at the company and help the employees invest in their plan and understand how their 401(k) plan works. Get some RFPs (Request for Proposals) and have your financial advisor help you compare all the different retirement plans and your options.

Q: Where should I put my extra cash I have from my business?

A: It depends what you want the cash for. If the liquid money is to pay taxes you may want to put it in a money market account. A money market account is like a savings account, so you can get at it easily, but you are generally earning a bit more interest. If you have extra cash you want to use to help you with your cash flow, a money market account may also be the best option. If you want to put the money away for the longer term you could use these dollars to help set up a retirement plan for the business, which would benefit you and your employees. You could also give the money to your employees as a bonus or you could set up a profit-sharing plan, which is not only a benefit to your employees, but a business expense that could help you on taxes.

INSURANCE

Q: How can I get help with insurance for my business?
A: Group benefits are so specific to each situation, so I truly recommend sitting down with an independent financial advisor or independent insurance agent to look at what benefits you have already set up, if any, and to take an assessment and determine all your options. You want someone who is independent and specializes in insurance; they can give you a complete assessment of your business, tell you what your options are in terms of health, life, disability and long-term care insurance, and help you compare them in terms of cost and best benefit to your business. Independence is key here because you want an unbiased opinion on all the plans and options available.

Q: How can I get a group health insurance plan? Are they a better deal than an individual health insurance policy?
A: Yes, group plans are usually the less expensive option of the two. Best of all, you only need two people to be a group, so if you own your own business and have just one employee besides yourself – who can be a family member or a spouse – you can set up a group plan.

Q: I'm quitting my job and starting a business. I'm worried that I will not have any benefits for a while. Any recommendations?

A: Among the benefits you may be giving up are: health insurance, dental insurance, life insurance, disability insurance, and a retirement plan. Trying to figure out what to do in this case can be tricky, because you need to know what your options are and cut expenses where you can, but make sure you don't set yourself up with liability that you can't handle. I generally recommend working on starting a business while you are working. If you do start the business after you've quit, at a minimum you want to get health insurance right away.

For health insurance, large companies offer COBRA, which is the same plan you had with your employer, but you pay the entire cost of the premiums, which can be expensive. You can have COBRA coverage for up to eighteen months; if you get divorced you can stay on your ex-spouse's COBRA for thirty-six months. But you should also look into getting your own health insurance policy in the meantime. It may be less expensive than COBRA because you have more control over the costs and the type of policy (for example, you might choose a higher deductible to keep your premiums lower). Equally important, having your own health insurance policy in place will help in case something happens to you healthwise that makes you uninsurable. That way you don't risk having none at all if you can't get insured when your COBRA runs out. Another option is to set up a group health insurance plan through your business, which you can do with only two employees (including an employee who's a spouse or family member).

You may also want to buy your own life insurance policy, especially if you have children or other people who depend on your income. Disability insurance replaces some of your income if you are disabled, but you can't buy a disability policy if you have no income.

Retirement benefits will stop until you are able to set up your own 401(k) plan or a SEP IRA. You can still contribute to a Traditional or Roth

IRA for yourself until you get a plan set up for the business. You will want to take your old 401(k) plan and roll it over into a Traditional IRA.

SUCCESSION PLANNING

Q: What is a buy-sell agreement?

A: A buy-sell agreement is a legal document for your business that helps answer some of the many "what if" questions. What if there is a death of a partner? What if there is a divorce? What if a partner becomes disabled? A buy-sell is an important document to have in place, along with the insurance necessary to protect the owners and the business. I had a client in a business partnership who passed away. There was a buy-sell agreement in place which was funded with life insurance, so when this partner passed away, the life insurance money went to the other partner to allow the business to buy out the spouse. The business stayed intact and the spouse still got a benefit.

Q: Is there a way to make sure my kids will inherit my business?

A: You can have legal documents set up to help protect yourself and your family. Among your choices are a buy-sell agreement or trust accounts. I would recommend sitting down with an estate planning attorney who can advise you and help you put everything in place for the specific way you want to the business to pass on to your kids, whether you're retiring or just getting out of the business.

Q: How do I get my money out of my business when I want to retire?

A: A buy-sell agreement can help you plan for this. Another option (among many) is to set up an ESOP – an employee stock ownership plan – where your employees buy shares of the business; that way you are transferring the shares you own to your employees. They pay you (for something of value – shares in the business!), while you get your money out of the business. You also could sell your business to another company, your partner, or another individual. The most important thing is to plan for your retirement before you get close to the date.

DIVORCE

Divorce is one of the most difficult transitions you can go through. Not only is it emotionally wrenching, it's a time when you really need to know everything about your financial situation so you can make decisions you're completely confident of and comfortable with. Money can be an emotional issue under the best circumstances; it can be even harder under stressful conditions like this, so it's even more crucial to separate your emotions from your finances and look at each asset as an asset. The doll, or baseball card, collection that you have had since you were a young child is a collection worth a certain dollar amount. It's not worth fighting over it because of an emotional issue.

You don't have to go through the divorce alone. Use community resources and professionals who deal with divorce every day – the attorneys, psychologists, financial advisors, and CPAs who specialize in divorce and know the ins and outs of the process. You also don't want to make decisions based solely on what your friends and family think you should do – you need to do what you think is right. Professionals can help you understand all your options. Then trust your own judgment and instincts to make the final decision – this is your life and your finances. If the only thing you take away from this chapter is to learn how to educate yourself, get organized, and ask for help, you will be on your way to achieving financial independence.

BEFORE THE DIVORCE BEGINS

Q: My spouse and I are separated right now and I am considering a divorce. What are some things I should consider about the financial aspects of divorce?

A: First, know that "divorce" is a word that does not have to destroy your financial future. There are four things you'll need to financially survive divorce: a place to live, little or no debt, retirement assets, and liquid money. You should strive for a balance of each of these – you need a mix, not an abundance in one category and none in the others. Next, remember that divorce itself is not a taxable event; it is what you do with the assets after the divorce that can affect you for the rest of your life.

Q: How do I know if I can even afford to get divorced?

A: Make a list of all of your assets and liabilities and meet with a Certified Divorce Financial Analyst (CDFA) to help you make that decision. As a CDFA, I have even helped couples decide if it makes more sense to go through the divorce or do a legal separation. If you are considering divorce, from a financial standpoint the first thing you need to do is figure out your total **marital net worth**. "Marital net worth" is the total of all of your assets and liabilities as a married couple. Then take all of these assets and debts to develop a balance sheet so you can pick the assets and liabilities that make the most sense for you now and in the future. A CDFA then can help you assess your situation. We look at which assets and liabilities you should take from the divorce and how they will affect you in the next year, in three years, five years, ten years and twenty years. Then we can walk you through your options, including how to pay for the divorce.

Q: I am just starting the divorce process. What should I be doing?

A: Start accumulating statements for any accounts you may have, such as investments, credit cards, car loans, mortgages, etc. After you have made copies of your account statements and have gathered a list of all your assets and liabilities, then you want to start working on your budget. Developing a budget is one of the most time-consuming and draining activities but it is imperative to do it, even more so if you will need spousal maintenance (alimony). Having a budget will also help you plan and make the decisions about which assets you should take as part of the divorce. You can find a budget worksheet on our website at www.helpingyouinvest. com. I'd also carry around a small notebook and just start writing down everything that you spend your money on; it's a little easier to develop a budget as you go along instead of trying to look back the last year through receipts, credit card statements, and even your checkbook.

Q: What are some of the most common mistakes you can make in going through a divorce?

A: There are many, but one of the first is not seeking guidance from qualified professionals. You don't want to leave everything up to your spouse. Another one is not understanding your complete financial picture. You can prepare yourself for the divorce by gathering all the financial records you can: You should have copies of brokerage account statements, retirement accounts, insurance, Social Security, mortgage statements, tax returns, and any other financial related documents. Still another is not getting your financial affairs in order. Make sure you close credit card accounts with a zero balance and start establishing your own credit. If you don't already have a checking and savings account in your own name, now's the time to get one. You should also make sure you have a credit card in your own name. Then take care of all those things you have been putting off: doctor appointments, car maintenance, making sure you have appropriate clothing in case you need to go on job interviews, etc. Do anything and everything so that you are not financially vulnerable. The biggest mistake women often made is becoming "house poor" – taking the house and nothing else. Don't do this. It does not make sense to stay in the home if you can't afford the mortgage or lifestyle that goes with owning the house, while in return you're giving up retirement accounts, which may be more valuable. You want to find the balance that will work for you and your financial plan for the future.

Q: What are some things I can do to keep my fees down in a divorce?

A: This list is not exhaustive, but here are some of my top recommendations:

- Be concise on the phone with your attorney. Write down all your questions and when you have a full list then call your attorney rather then calling with just one question.
- Find documents and gather as much information as you can yourself.
- Make copies and organize your files yourself.
- Don't use your attorney as your therapist. Talk to friends, join a support group, or hire a therapist to help you with your emotions.
- If you are able to divide IRAs do so rather than dividing 401(k)s. You don't need a QDRO (see below) to divide IRAs, but you do for a 401(k), and they cost money.
- If you need help doing your budget, figuring out what assets you should take or even understanding your financial picture, hire a Certified

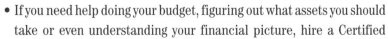

> $
>
> # Money Tip:
>
> There are four things financially you need to survive a divorce:
>
> - Liquid money
> - Retirement assets
> - A place to live
> - Little or no debt

Divorce Financial Analyst. In the long run it should save you some time and money, and will help you stay in control with your money.

Q: I have heard there are many different ways to go through the divorce process, including Collaborative Divorce. What is this?

A: Collaborative law is a process where you and your spouse each have an attorney and you agree not to go to trial. You share information back and forth and work on your divorce together to bring about a win-win situation. The Collaborative Law Institute is made up of professionals in the family law area who focus on helping individuals through the divorce process with their needs at the forefront rather than the needs of the attorney or other outside parties; you can visit them at www.collaborativelaw.org. There's also Collaborative Team Divorce where coaches and financial professionals like me come into the process to help facilitate your divorce. This team of professionals works with you and your partner rather than pitting the two of you against each other. Collaborative Team Divorce is especially great for couples who want to work together; if you have kids, it's a great way to put the kids first. You also don't have to do a full Collaborative Team Divorce. I have had many cases where a husband and wife come to me and I help them divide their financial assets, then they go to an attorney to have the divorce decree drawn up.

ASSETS vs. LIABILITIES

Q: What are assets and liabilities?

A: Take out a sheet of paper and develop a list of all the things you own (your assets) and all the debts you have (your liabilities).

There are many different types of assets: Some assets appreciate, or could increase in value, while others, such as a car or personal property, are depreciating assets, which are generally worth less than what you paid after you've had them for a short time. Some assets have growth potential. Assets that can grow are things like stocks, CDs, or even money sitting in a money market account. These assets could appreciate in value over time rather than lose value over time.

Some assets are more liquid than others – you can get at them as cash more easily, such as funds sitting in a money market account, a savings account, or even your checking account. Some assets are also income generating – that is, they'll help keep some money coming in – such as stocks that pay dividends or rental property with positive cash flow (it's not costing you more in taxes and maintenance costs than what you get from it in rent). Even debts come in different types; for example, some debts have interest you can deduct, others don't.

Q: Is it best just to divide the assets and liabilities equally?

A: Not necessarily. You might want to take your own IRA and your ex might take his/her own IRA. The most important thing is to understand the big picture. Think of your divorce settlement as a puzzle; it's an assessment of your overall situation, then you need to pick and choose which assets and/or liabilities make the most sense for you in your situation now and in the future.

It's also important to realize that assets or liabilities sitting next to each other on a balance sheet are not necessarily equal. Think about this example for a minute: Suppose you have $10,000 sitting in your money market account, and $10,000 worth of ABC stock that you purchased back in 1997 for $2,000. It may seem that both assets are equal, but they're really not. If you go ahead and sell that ABC stock, you'll end up with a capital gain of $8,000 and will have to pay taxes on it. Stock is not liquid – you have to sell it in order to get at the cash. Whereas you can access the money immediately in your money market account because it's liquid.

Q: I'm going through a divorce; we have a $25,000 home equity loan and a credit card with a $20,000 balance on it. Which liability should I take?

A: Generally, a liability follows the asset, so if you are taking the house you will end up with the home equity loan. This might actually be the liability that you want, though. It's $5,000 more, but the interest rate may well be lower than the rate for the credit card, plus the interest is tax-deductible. You have to be sure that taking the house makes sense for you in other ways as well, though, because it's the way you can choose this liability. It's important to run your credit every year, but even more so when you're going through a divorce, because the report will tell you what liabilities you have that are jointly held and those that are held just in your name. You can go to www.annualcreditreport.com to get a copy of your report. Then you want to analyze the debts that you do have so you can pick those that make the most sense for you. Some factors you'll want to consider are whether the interest on the debt is deductible, what the interest rate is, and whose name the debt is in.

Q: I have a car that isn't worth anything, while my husband leases his car. Why is mine on our balance sheet and my husband's isn't?

A: If you lease a vehicle there is no value to the car. It is not an asset and it is not a liability. When you own a car what goes on the balance sheet is what the car is worth minus anything you may owe on the car. You can find out what your car is worth is by going to the Kelley Blue Book either at your library or online at www.kbb.com. Subtract what you owe and that's your equity in your car. It's even possible that you owe more on your car than it is worth, which unfortunately makes it a liability.

Q: What is marital and non-marital property?

A: It's an important concept to understand. **Marital assets**, or **marital property**, are the assets that you have accumulated together during the marriage. **Non-marital property** could be assets such as an inheritance that is still in your name only, which generally do not go on the balance sheet to be divided.

If you took the money in the inheritance and paid off some debt, bought a car, or invested the money in a joint account, however, it could lose its non-marital claim. Check with your attorney because each state has different regulations on divorce and how assets are treated in a divorce.

THE FOUR THINGS YOU NEED . . .

Q: You mentioned the four things I need financially to survive a divorce. Can you expand on this?

A: Yes. These four things are a place to live, little or no debt, liquid money, and retirement assets or the means to accumulate retirement assets.

1. A PLACE TO LIVE

We all need a place to live, but when you're in a life transition such as divorce, it's imperative that you look at the financial ramifications of every choice. You have many options: staying in your current home, buying a different home, renting for a short time or moving in with a friend. Whatever you decide, you need to be able to afford the place from a cash-flow standpoint – that is, you need to have enough money every month to cover the mortgage, taxes, maintenance, etc.

Q: I've got kids and everything is so crazy right now – would it be best to stay in my house?

A: I see so many people taking the house because of kids and a general desire for stability during a tough time. I understand completely – but how stable are you if you take the house, then can't afford the payments later? A house is not a liquid asset and if you look historically at the stock market, a house may have less appreciation potential compared with money set aside for retirement.

It's also a mistake to take the house because you feel attached to it; this is a time when you have to do the hard work of separating your emotions from your finances. Choose the assets from the divorce that make the most sense for you. It could be better to rent for a short time or to purchase a less expensive home.

Q: OK, I've made the tough but smart choice and decided to sell the house. Is it better to sell right away and get it over with, or wait and see if it rises on the market?

A: It might make the most sense from a tax standpoint to sell the house while still married rather than take the house and sell as a single person a few years later. In 1997, the tax code changed relating to home ownership. A married couple can exclude up to $500,000 of capital gains on a home sale and a single person can exclude up to $250,000 as long you have lived in the home for two out of the last five years. (Your capital gain is the bottom-line profit you end up with after real estate agent fees, any improvements you have made to your home, any liabilities, and any other house expenses.) What this means is that if you take the house as part of the divorce and sell it a year later with a gain of over $250,000 you will pay capital gains taxes. On the other hand, if you sold the house pursuant to the divorce and had a capital gain of less than $500,000 there would have been no taxable gain. Let's say you bought a house in 1975 for $200,000. Today it's worth $600,000 and you sell the house as part of the divorce while you are married. You'll have a gain of $400,000 but you wouldn't have to pay capital gains taxes. (You're still under the $500,000 exclusion for couples.) If you took the house as part of the divorce and sold it a year later, as a single person, for $400,000, you only have an exclusion of $250,000. That means you'd have to pay capital gains taxes on $150,000 ($400,00 - $250,000 = $150,000).

Q: I am getting a divorce and am moving out of the house. Do I wait to buy new furniture or how do we split up our personal property?

A: Generally, personal property does not go on your balance sheet to be divided. Look to see what personal property items you already have and how you can divide them so you both feel good about the division. One suggestion is to buy the new items you need with marital funds rather than waiting until the divorce is over to buy these items with your own money. But proceed with caution, because divorce is expensive and it costs more money to run two households than one. If you are short on liquid money, this is going to be especially difficult.

2. LITTLE OR NO DEBT

It is ideal to walk away from the divorce with no debt, but that's often hard to do. Because there is a high cost to having debt, you need to know the difference between good debt and bad debt. Good debt is a mortgage, student loan or some sort of investment in yourself or your future. Bad debt is basically everything else, including credit cards or personal loans. Remember that in divorce, generally a liability will follow the asset. In other words, the car loan will usually follow the car; the home equity line or loan will follow the house. Generally, it's best to get rid of the bad debts during the divorce. If it makes sense liquidate some assets, such as selling some stocks, cashing in some CDs, or selling a car to pay off the bad debt.

Q: What if my spouse has a credit card in my name or we have a joint credit card?

A: The creditor wants the debt paid regardless of the situation. Your divorce decree is separate from your agreement with the credit card company, and the credit card company doesn't care what the divorce decree says. So if your spouse takes a credit card with your name on it and does not pay that debt, the creditor will come after you. This will happen even with a joint account. If your spouse is financially responsible now, generally they will remain responsible after the divorce. If your spouse is not financially responsible now, a divorce is not going to make him or her responsible.

Q: I worry that my soon-to-be ex-spouse will not keep up with the payments on our joint card after the divorce. What should I do?
A: One solution is to take all the debt yourself. This might sound scary or crazy, especially if it's a large amount of debt, but because you're taking more debt with the divorce you can then bargain for more assets in the divorce agreement to equalize your property settlement. Another possibility is to call the credit card company and see if they will close your joint account and open up two new accounts. Say, for example, you had $12,000 on your joint card; in this case one account would be in your name with a $6,000 balance and one would be for your spouse with a $6,000 balance and your joint account would be closed.

Q: I was divorced three years ago and as part of the divorce my husband (now ex) took the $9,000 on our joint credit cards. He has not paid the bill and now the creditors are calling me. What do I do?
A: Unfortunately this is one question that I get too often. You will want to pay the debt to save your credit and then you will become a creditor of your spouse. This means you will need to get an attorney to help you collect the money. This is yet another reason why you need to carefully consider whether it's worth it to take on big liabilities in exchange for more assets.

Q: I have a joint line of credit with my spouse. Should I be worried if we get a divorce?
A: You know your spouse better than anyone else, so you don't necessarily have to be worried – but you do want to protect yourself and your credit.

If you have a line of credit of $50,000 available and you are not using any of the money, be aware that as a joint line of credit either one of you has access to the money. You may want to write a letter to the bank or credit union letting them know you are thinking of a divorce or in the middle of a divorce. This could help, but the best option is to close out the line to limit your exposure. I would only do this if you definitely don't need access to the money, though.

Q: I don't have any credit cards in my own name and I am getting a divorce. Should I get some credit cards?
A: Yes. If you don't have a credit card or a checking account in your own name you definitely want to get one. You need credit in your own name, so you can establish a good credit history. You can do this by getting a credit card and charging a small amount every month – for instance, gas for your car – and paying it off in full and on time every month.

Q: I have some credit cards in my name that I haven't used for a long time. What should I do with them?
A: If they are credit cards that have a zero balance, call and cancel those cards. You want to clean up any debts during the divorce to limit your liability after the divorce. Part of your score is made up of your credit history and you also don't want to limit your access to credit, especially with a divorce. So make certain these are cards you will never need or use again.

3. RETIREMENT ASSETS

Retirement assets can take many forms, so make sure you don't forget any and leave money on the table. Retirement plans are required to send a year-end statement at the end of every year, so gather them from all the retirement accounts you or your spouse have. The statements will generally come from the retirement plan provider, not you or your spouse's direct employer. They could include 401(k)s, 403(b)s, and 457 plans; if there is a small business involved there could be SEP or SIMPLE IRA. Also check for any pension plan statements, statements of stock options, or ESOPs (employee stock ownership plans) that you or your spouse may have through work. You and/or your spouse may have Roth and Traditional IRA accounts as well.

Q: What's a QDRO?

A: QDRO stands for qualified domestic relations order. It's a legal document an attorney draws up that is separate from your divorce decree. It's generally needed for retirement plans that are part of an employer's retirement plan, such as a 401(k); it takes the retirement accounts and transfers them pursuant to your divorce decree. This document is sent to the benefits department of the 401(k) plan provider to instruct them on how to divide the assets. Make sure the QDRO is written correctly BEFORE the divorce is final to ensure that you receive your retirement assets from your spouse's plan. A QDRO is *not* needed to divide IRAs, so if you have an old 401(k) plan you may want to roll it over to a Traditional IRA. This will save you money, because it costs to have an attorney draw up the QDRO.

Q: What should I do if the benefit plan can't be divided?

A: In this case, you want to look at other assets of the marriage and receive those instead. For example, if a pension cannot be divided, take more of the 401(k) assets of your spouse. You can take the 401(k) and roll it into a Traditional IRA in your own name.

Q: What about IRAs? How do we separate those?

A: First, figure out whether they are a Roth IRA, Traditional IRA, or whether there are both types of accounts. It's also possible there are more than one account of any of these types. If you receive retirement assets from your spouse's IRA, you will need a copy of your divorce decree and a few other financial forms to separate those assets. You should change the account into your name by rolling the assets into your IRA account. This process is known as a "direct rollover." It's among the many compelling reasons to have a financial plan in place as the foundation for your financial future, and to have a financial advisor help you transfer and invest these assets for you based on your retirement goals and needs.

Q: What happens with Social Security in my divorce?
A: If you've been married at least ten years, then get divorced, you can collect your own Social Security or half of your spouse's, whichever is greater. This has no effect on your ex-spouse – he or she will still receive the same dollar amount they would have regardless. So let's say your Social Security at retirement is $300 a month, and your spouse's is $1,800 a month; you could take $300 a month or $900 a month. Obviously, you'll take the $900 a month, and your ex-spouse will still get his or her same $1,800 a month. This is Social Security law and does not go in your divorce decree. However, be aware that the laws governing Social Security can change at any time.

Q: I have heard it's possible to take money out of a 401(k) without the 10 percent penalty because I'm going through a divorce. Is this true?
A: Yes. It is a section of the tax code called 72(t)(2)c. You are allowed to take money out of your spouse's 401(k) plan and escape the 10 percent penalty even if you are under the age of 59½ if it is pursuant to a divorce. You still have to pay state and federal income taxes on the money, though. This is one way spouses can get liquid money if there is no better option out of the divorce. This only works on 401(k) plans that belong to your spouse (or soon-to-be ex). It does not work with IRAs.

4. LIQUID MONEY

There are three different general phases of the divorce process: the beginning, middle, and after (the post-divorce phase). In each of these stages, your budget may be different, so make sure you have liquid money available at all times. This may seem like an insurmountable obstacle but you'll need liquid money to cover the cost of the divorce and to maintain your lifestyle during the divorce process. In the beginning, you'll need liquid money for the retainer to hire an attorney. You should consider putting this in a money market account rather than a savings or checking account because you'll earn more interest on it. For the post-divorce phase, you may need liquid money if your ex is not paying child support or spousal maintenance on time. You'll also need liquid money in case of an emergency – if you lose your job, you have a child emergency, health care crisis, etc.

Q: I don't have very much liquid money right now. What should I do?
A: First, try not to stress about it too much. In the beginning and during the divorce, just meet your expenses as best you can. It's often very difficult to accumulate liquid money at this point; the important thing is to make it financially from a cash-flow standpoint through the divorce and focus on getting some liquid dollars as part of the divorce settlement. But make absolutely sure as part of the divorce settlement that you have liquid money or the means to build up some liquid funds when the divorce is over. Coming out of the divorce process without enough liquid money or the means to save is one of the biggest mistakes I see.

Q: I'm really broke. Is there a way I can get some liquid money just to meet expenses with the divorce?
A: As a very, very last resort, you can withdraw from a 401(k) without penalty pursuant to a divorce if you are receiving your ex-spouse's 401(k)

as part of the divorce. You still will pay state and federal income taxes on these dollars. However, I generally have had couples use equity in their homes if available, if interest rates have been low and it makes sense from a cash-flow standpoint. You can use credit cards, seek out a personal loan or if possible work with your spouse on a budget to help you manage.

Q: I found out that I have $50,000 in credit card bills, IRS debt of $35,000 and a lien against my home. I want a divorce. I don't want to mess this up. Is there anything I should do or know?
A: Your question is one of the reasons I do what I do. So many of us used to (and sometimes still do) ignore any conversation or any issue relating to money. If you're in a relationship it's important to share and use each person's strengths to make for a financially strong unit. If you suddenly find yourself in a financial situation that you didn't know about, the first thing to do is to gain control by gathering information. To assess your financial situation from a liability standpoint I would get a copy of your credit report. I'd also call your accountant if you have one or call the IRS and get copies of you tax returns for at least the last five years. Between these documents you can at least gather some information to assess your situation. I also would contact an attorney to help you understand your options.

Q: I have an attorney bill that is thousands and thousands of dollars. How can I get back on my feet?
A: This is one of the many reasons I recommend coming out of the divorce process with some liquid money, or at least the means to accumulate some. You especially need liquid money to pay off any liabilities arising from the divorce (such as this attorney's bill). If you don't already have a plan for your overall financial situation, start working on one. Then talk to your attorney – you may be able to refinance the debt or get on a payment plan. Whatever you do, don't ignore their requests for payment.

CHILD SUPPORT AND SPOUSAL MAINTENANCE

Q: I am paying my ex-wife money child support every month. Can I deduct this on my taxes?
A: No, you cannot deduct child support. Child support is not taxable income for the person receiving it. Child support is the money needed to care for the child.

Q: How much child support can I expect?
A: It depends on the state where you live. Some states have formulas and some have guidelines. This is where you should work with your attorney and your financial advisor to help you develop your budget and get an assessment of your situation. Just remember that child support is not taxable for the recipient and not deductible to the payer.

Q: Can I deduct the spousal maintenance that I have to pay my ex-spouse?
A: Spousal maintenance, otherwise known as alimony, is tax-deductible for the person paying and is taxable income for those receiving it.

Q: How much spousal maintenance can I be expected to pay my soon-to-be ex?
A: There are no guidelines or formulas for spousal maintenance. It depends on your income, your expenses, and the income and expenses of your spouse.

Q: My husband wants to pay me only $200 a month in spousal maintenance but I need $1,900 a month. How can we come to an agreement?
A: This is where a Certified Divorce Financial Analyst can help you with projections and cash-flow analysis to determine an accurate dollar amount and what is realistic. You want to consider how much money you have coming in and going out every month; your spouse needs to do the

same. This is why it's so important to have a budget in place – spend your time and energy on your budget, not on fighting over a "right" or "unfair" dollar amount. Also make sure you consider taxes. Spousal maintenance is taxable, so if your budget does show you need exactly $1,900 a month for expenses, include additional dollars every month to cover the state and federal income taxes for that amount.

INSURANCE

Q: I'm the beneficiary of a life insurance policy on my husband (soon to be ex). Will I remain the beneficiary?
A: You will remain the beneficiary if you negotiate this as part of the divorce. There is nothing wrong with remaining the beneficiary but you do want to know what kind of policy it is, how much the premiums are, and if you're responsible for those.

Q: Do I need life insurance on my ex?
A: It's possible that you do. One of the most common mistakes I see people make with the divorce process is not having any life insurance as part of the divorce; it's crucial to have some if you're dependent on your ex-spouse for spousal maintenance or child support. Some advisors suggest taking out a new life insurance policy on your ex before the divorce is finalized so that you own the policy and you make the premium payments. This way you never have to wonder if you are still the beneficiary, or if the payments are being made to keep the policy in force. Generally, a term life insurance policy is inexpensive and can be taken out for ten to twenty years just to cover the period during which you'll be relying on this money from your ex-spouse.

Q: I don't work and right now and I'm covered under my husband's health insurance plan. What do I do about health insurance when I'm divorced?

A: Make sure you include the cost of health insurance when you're developing your budget. You can go on COBRA, from your ex-spouse's employer, for up to thirty-six months, or you could get your own health insurance policy if you don't have coverage through your employer. It might be less expensive to purchase your own health insurance policy than going on COBRA; you may be able to get a policy with a higher deductible and/or your policy would be based upon your own health history rather than being part of a group. Another good reason to buy your own health insurance policy is to make sure you'll always have some insurance. If something happens to you while you're on COBRA and you have no other health insurance, you could find yourself uninsurable when COBRA runs out.

Q: I have heard that when my divorce is over that's really when the work starts. What does this mean?

A: I know the divorce process is so stressful in itself that it's tempting to just let things fall by the wayside once the legal documents are signed. It's hard, but don't give in to this temptation. Find a financial advisor to help you take the assets that may have been divided during the divorce and transfer them correctly into your name. Among the things you'll want to take care of are making sure you escape any unnecessary charges. For instance, you can take the retirement assets and roll them over into your own IRA. You'll also want to immediately change the beneficiaries of any accounts that you have open such as your 401(k), IRAs, and even life insurance. You may also want to consider getting a new will.

KIDS AND MONEY

Credit Cards and Scores   Business Ownership   Protecting your Assets   Kids and Money   Divorce   Identity Theft   Budgeting   Banking   Money Coming and Going   Investing 101   Credit Cards and Scores   Protecting Assets   Kids and Money   Divorce   Identity Theft   Budgeting   Money Coming and Going   Investing   Credit Cards and Scores   Protecting your Assets   Kids and Money   Divorce   Identity Theft   Budgeting   Money Coming and Going   Investing 101   Credit Cards and Scores   Protecting your Assets   Kids and Money   Divorce   Identity Theft   Banking   Money Coming and Going   Investing 101   Credit Cards and Scores   Protecting your Assets   Kids and Money   Divorce   Identity Theft   Budgeting   Money Coming and Going   Investing 101   Credit Cards and Scores   Protecting your Assets   Kids and Money   Divorce   Identity Theft   Budgeting   Money Coming and Going   Investing 101   Credit Cards and Scores   Protecting your Assets   Kids and Money   Divorce   Identity Theft   Budgeting   Money Coming and Going   Investing 101   Credit Cards and Scores

How you think, feel, spend, and save your money has a correlation to how you were raised and the memories you have of money. You may have grown up being told that money doesn't grow on trees; is your child growing up learning that money does not just magically come out of ATMs? Teaching our children how to save and spend wisely is one of the most important things we can do, and one of the best ways to teach our kids about money is to be a great example.

Kids are very observant. They watch us spend money, but how often do they see us save or invest money? They get so many messages to spend – from television ads, magazine ads, billboards, and from peer pressure to get the latest electronic gadget their friends have. But how many messages are we giving our kids to save or invest?

The first thing to do is to realize where you are spending and investing your own money; then you can help your kids. Keeping your kids involved and having a goal that's important to them can get them excited about saving. The satisfaction they receive from achieving their goals can help create good saving and spending habits for the rest of their lives. The questions and answers that follow will give you some guidelines for being a good role model for the kids in your life and helping them work towards financial independence.

MONEY-WISE KIDS

Q: What are some things I can do to teach my kids how to save and spend wisely?

A: One of the greatest ways to teach our kids about money is to practice what you preach. Sit down together and set goals together with your kids. This way they're saving towards something that matters to them, while they see you saving to achieve your goals. You can take your child to the bank or a meeting with your financial advisor. If your child watches you at the bank and watches you go to meetings with your financial advisor they will learn from you the importance of saving and investing in a way that no amount of simply telling them can match.

Q: My child is seven and I'm wondering if it's too early to start talking to her about money?

A: The earlier money lessons are learned, the better. The benefits are both short- and long-term. You can work with your kids as soon as they start asking for something. You are learning – or have learned – to take what's important in your life and attach that to your money; you can use this same tool to help teach your kids about money. Let's say your child wants a certain toy. Set a goal for them, for example, an achievement at school. If they accomplish that goal, they get the toy. Better yet, have them save for half of the item as well.

When you go to the cash machine, explain to your child how it works. If you feel comfortable, show her one of your paychecks and explain how many hours you worked, how much is taken out for taxes and how much is taken out for your 401(k). You can also talk to your seven-year-old about their experiences with money. And always look for daily events that can help shape your child's memories about money. Every day the opportunities are endless to make new money memories.

ALLOWANCES, SAVING, AND INVESTING

Q: Should I give my child an allowance? If so, how much?

A: I always encourage parents to give their kids an allowance. It's not so much the dollar amount you're giving them, it's the underlying principles and the money memories you're instilling in your kids. One way to figure out a specific amount is to take all the money you spend every week on "Mom, can I have this?" or "Dad, can I have that?" Add it up, divide in half, and give that amount to your child as their allowance. You'll not only save yourself some money but you'll be teaching your child about money.

Don't be afraid to follow the same advice for yourself. Take all the money you spend today on coffee, snacks, lunch, a new book you wanted, and all those other extras. Add it all up, divide it in half and give yourself those dollars as an allowance. It's a great example to set.

Q: Is it too soon to start giving an allowance to a six-year-old?

A: No, it isn't too soon. Giving an allowance can be a great opportunity for teaching important financial lessons. Even very young children can begin to understand the concept of earning money. Explain to your children that money is earned by working and that you can only spend what you earn. To help your child understand what it's like to get paid on a schedule, begin "paying" your children an allowance. Help your children set goals for how they spend and save their allowance, making sure that you as parents stick to the payment schedule – otherwise the lesson may be lost.

As kids get into middle or high school, I've seen some of my clients buy a jacket, shoes and jeans for their kids every year; then the kids are responsible for anything beyond that. This empowers your kids with their money and helps them learn how to make wise choices with money.

Q: How can I encourage my child to understand that money isn't just about buying things now?

A: Once your child starts getting an allowance, help them divide it into three piggy banks. The money in one bank they can spend on whatever they want. Money from the second bank goes to charity. It helps if the child can pick out a charity that means something to them personally, like the Animal Humane Society or a charity they know will help a person in need at their school. The money in the third piggy bank will be savings for the future.

Q: Every time I take my child to a store he always has a fit about some item he just HAS to have. I don't want to waste my money and I can't afford to buy him everything he wants. What do I do?

A: "Buy me this." "I want that." What parent hasn't heard these phrases from their children? You can teach your children an important lesson about saving and setting goals *and* get rid of the "I want" and "Buy this" all the time by encouraging them to save a portion of their allowance or other money they have to achieve a "special" goal. Teaching your children about responsible saving may seem daunting at first, but you can help put your child on the right track in the future by developing smart habits now. To this day I still set goals for myself for saving so that I can achieve my "special" goals as well.

Q: So how do I set financial goals with my kids?

A: Sit down with them and figure out what they feel is worth saving (and waiting) for. You can set yourself a goal at the same time, so they also see you saving to achieve your goals. You want to make your goals specific, so pick a specific item and a specific time-line. The most important thing is to follow through, so if/when the goal is achieved the reward actually happens. After you've set some goals, go to the bank together and help your child set up a savings account. As your child gets older you could have them meet with your financial advisor to set up an account to save for college or even set up a Roth IRA.

Q: Have you heard any stories of children who had early financial education who are financially successful adults?
A: Yes, I have. I have clients who have brought their kids in to their appointments with me and help their kids set up a Roth IRA. These kids then go onto college and realize the importance of saving money rather than spending every cent they have (or even don't have) today. I've known of other kids who have started businesses while still in their childhood years because their parents have instilled the values of saving, investing, and buying assets. And raising financially savvy kids has an extra benefit: It's a great confidence-builder too.

Q: I want to start teaching my seven-year-old daughter about investing. Is this an appropriate age to start? If so, any suggestions?
A: It's appropriate as soon as kids start asking about something related to money or ask for an item that costs money. Set up a custodial account – an account in your child's name and your name. You can deposit some money, then you can invest these dollars in an individual stock that your child can get excited about. You could help your child pick a stock that has to do with something he/she is interested in, starting by offering your child a choice of stocks. Then you can show your child how to view their account online and watch the stock chart. You can explain how a stock works and why prices go up and down.

I would also set up a family 401(k). With a family 401(k), you as a family come up with a goal for your money; you as a parent can offer a matching program. The goal could be a pool, a trip, or a new "toy" for the family, like a video game. So, for example, if your daughter puts in $1 to the family 401(k), you could match her 50 cents. This way she can learn about 401(k)s so when she starts her first job she understands the concept of the 401(k) and the concept of investing. There is no price you can put on this kind of education.

Q: My child worked during the summer and earned about $1,200. I would like to help her save for the future. What do I do?

A: Good for you – it's never too early for you and your child to start thinking about the future! Children with earned income may contribute to either a Traditional IRA or a Roth IRA. Your child can contribute as much as they earn in either IRA, so in this case, he or she could put $1,200 in a Roth or Traditional IRA for this year. With a Roth IRA your child can withdraw in their own retirement all or part of their contributions without any income tax or penalty. If they take the money out before they're 59½ years old, they can withdraw up to $10,000 income-tax free to pay for college or a down payment on a house. Owning a Roth or Traditional IRA will not cost your child any financial aid dollars at college time either, according to current guidelines, because the financial aid calculations don't count IRAs as assets.

Q: My teenage son now has a job, and I want to help him save money. Where should I help him put his money?

A: First see if his employer offers a retirement plan and if your son is eligible. Otherwise, you could consider a Roth or Traditional IRA (see previous question), Coverdell Education Savings Account (formerly known as an Education IRA) or even just a money market account, depending on what he's saving the money for. A Roth IRA is a retirement account, but the dollars can be used for college or a first-time home purchase up to $10,000 without penalty. Other restrictions, penalties, and taxes may apply. Unless certain criteria are met, Roth IRA owners must be 59½ or older and have held the IRA for five years before tax-free withdrawals are permitted.

MONEY-WISE PARENTS: RETIREMENT vs. COLLEGE

Q: How can we possibly get ahead with saving for college with the costs increasing so dramatically?

A: The Bureau of Labor Statistics reports that the tuition component of the Consumer Price Index (CPI) increased by 8 percent per year, on average, from 1979 to 2001. This means that children born today will face college costs several times greater than current prices. When you factor in the costs of room, board, and textbooks, it adds up to a hefty sum. But don't despair. If you start saving early enough, even a modest weekly or monthly investment can grow to a significant college fund by the time your child enrolls in college; remember, if you start when your child is a baby, you have almost 18 years. Just $500 a month from birth would yield about $200,000 by the time your child turns seventeen, assuming a 7 percent return on investment. Saving $200 a month would generate almost $80,000.

Q: I recently had a new baby and want to start saving for college but it would mean I wouldn't be putting away any money for retirement. Is this OK?

A: No, even though it seems to go against every parental instinct. Women especially tend to try to take care of others before taking care of themselves. Putting your kids first is fine if you're buying them a cute new outfit instead of something for yourself. However, if you start saving for their college instead of putting money away for your retirement this becomes a problem; you don't want to end up penniless in your "golden years" after you finish paying for their entire college education.

If this still seems hard to swallow, think about those airplane instructions where the flight attendant always tells you to make sure you have your oxygen mask on first before helping your children with theirs. The same rule applies financially. Remember that there are no loans for retirement but there are student loans for higher education. On a practical level, you should also remember the many tax advantages of the 401(k), Roth IRAs, and other accounts that you want to take advantage of. Finally, your child will probably be happier if they have to help pay for their education than pay for you in your retirement.

Q: I'm saving for my retirement; now I also want to start saving for my new child to be able to go to college. Where do I start?

A: Congratulations on your new little one and congratulations on wanting to save already for her higher education! A useful way to look at saving and helping children through college is the "third" rule: You save for a third of the tuition and expenses, you pay for a third of the tuition and expenses when they're in school, and you use financing and scholarships for the other third. This way it doesn't seem like such an overwhelming amount of money you have to save, plus it's easier to save for both your retirement and your children's education.

TYPES OF COLLEGE ACCOUNTS

Q: What are the best options for saving for my child's college education? I don't necessarily like putting it into a savings account that earns lousy interest.

A: You're right – I would steer away from a savings account because with the rise in college costs compared with the rates you'd earn on a savings account you could be losing money. Possibly a better option is a 529 plan or Coverdell Education Savings Account.

Q: What's the difference between a 529 plan and a Coverdell (also known as the Education IRA)?

A: One big difference is what you can use the money for. With a 529 plan you can withdraw the money tax-free on earnings and use it on most higher education expenses. With a Coverdell, the child doesn't have to pay taxes on the interest the account earns either, but the money needs to be used for higher education. Money in the Coverdell can be invested in almost anything – stocks, bonds, or other investment vehicles. The owner of the account, along with a financial advisor, decides where the money is invested. The 529 plan cannot be invested in individual stocks or CDs. The plan gives you options to choose from. In the Coverdell you can contribute up to $2,000 per year until the child is eighteen; most 529 plans allow you to put away up to a few hundred thousand in a year. In the Coverdell the money has to be used for education expenses by the time the beneficiary is thirty; there are no age restrictions with the 529. Talk to your financial advisor to see which one will work best for your family.

Q: Can I open a Coverdell account for my niece?

A: You sure can if you meet the requirements; your modified adjusted gross income needs to be less than $95,000 as a single tax filer or $190,000 as a married couple filing jointly in the tax year in which you contribute. A few things that aren't required: A contributor to a Coverdell doesn't have to have earned income; nor does the person who adds money to the account have to be related to the beneficiary. But a child can only have one Coverdell account so if the parents have opened one up for your niece, you couldn't. But you could add to the one they own as long as the contribution does not go above $2,000 each year. You also have until April 15th of every year to make contributions for the previous year.

Q: Do you recommend starting with a Coverdell or a 529?

A: I generally recommend starting with Coverdell. You can contribute up to $2,000 per year per child until the child is eighteen. In the Coverdell you can invest in anything and there is no set rate of return. You can be as aggressive or as conservative as you want. There are also no taxes with the

Coverdell account as long the money is used before the child is thirty and used for higher education expenses. However, a child can only have one Coverdell account whereas a child can have multiple 529 plans. Be sure to talk to your financial advisor, though, to make sure this general rule fits your specific situation.

Q: What is a 529 plan?

A: The 529 plan is named after a section of the tax code. These state-sponsored college savings programs offer generous tax breaks and other benefits. One option offers pre-paid tuition plans, which enable you to pay now, at today's tuition rates, for future enrollment. Another option enables you to save money in a tax-deferred account to be used to pay for education at future tuition rates. Some of the benefits of the 529 plan include:

- Generous contribution limits: Investment minimums are low. You can start with as little as $25 a month. There is no restriction on how much you contribute every year, though contributions of more than $12,000 are subject to the gift tax (more than $24,000 if contributing with a spouse). You can contribute up to about $230,000 into most 529 plans each year.

- Control: The account owner always has control of the money, which eliminates the possibility that the money could be used for anything other than higher education. In other words, Junior can't decide to take his college money and go to Cancun, because the money is in your name. Second, you, the owner, stay in control of the account. With few exceptions, the named beneficiary has no rights to the funds. You're the one who calls the shots; you decide when withdrawals are taken and for what purpose.

- Account flexibility: There are no restrictions on who can open an account for whom. You can open an account for your child, a grandchild or other relative, a friend's child, or even yourself.

- Open contributions: Anyone can contribute to the 529 plan. This resolves the annual dilemma of what to get a child for his or her birthday.
- There is no age restriction on the 529 plan. Everyone is eligible to take advantage of a 529 plan
- There are few if any income limitations.
- Your investment grows tax-deferred, and the distributions to pay for the beneficiary's college costs come out federally tax-free.

Finally, a 529 plan can provide a very easy hands-off way to save for college. Once you decide which 529 plan to use, you complete a simple enrollment form and make your contribution. You can make it even easier by signing up for automatic deposits. In some 529 plans, ongoing investment of your account is handled by the 529 plan, not by you. In these cases, plan assets are professionally managed either by the state treasurer's office or by an outside investment company hired as the program manager. Other 529 plans offer you choices on allocations with the plan. By investing in a 529 plan outside of the state in which you pay taxes you may lose tax benefits offered by the state's plan. Withdrawals used for qualified expenses are federally tax-free. Tax treatment at the state level may vary.

Q: My husband wants to open an account for our grandchildren to contribute towards their college education. He's talking about opening a 529 account. Is this good? What are the advantages or disadvantages?

A: A 529 plan is a great vehicle for grandparents because of gifting. Any person can gift money every year up to $12,000 a year per person without triggering gift tax, but only with the 529 plan can you speed that up for five years. What that means is that you as Grandma Jane can put $60,000 ($12,000 a year for five years) today in a 529 plan for your grandchild; your husband, Grandpa Jim, can also put $60,000 today. This has a double benefit: You have that money out of your estate, which could help you/your beneficiaries later lower taxes on your estate, and your grandchild now has the money in a 529, which can be invested and grow for their college education.

Q: What should I look for in figuring out which 529 plan to go with?
A: The first thing you need to do is start researching the various plans. There are many options, and each 529 plan has its own distinctions. Look for the investment strategies, tax benefits, and other incentives that best match your needs and the beneficiary's needs. Some 529 plans allow you to pick the specific investment options, while others only allow you to invest based on the child's age. Your home state might offer a 529 plan that has special advantages if you are a resident, such as a possible tax deduction.

WAYS TO SAVE FOR KIDS

Q: I have two kids already in college and one who'll be starting next year, and I am feeling really strapped. I heard I could take money out of my IRA without the 10 percent penalty to pay for their college. Is this true?
A: Yes, it is true that you can take money out of your IRA and escape the 10 percent penalty even if you're under the age 59½ but you still will pay state and federal income taxes. As always, drawing from your retirement is a last resort; you also need to make sure the money goes toward qualified schooling costs (for yourself, your spouse, or your children or grandkids) – that is, the eligible student attends an IRS-approved institution. This is any college, university, vocational school, or other post-secondary facility that meets federal student aid program requirements. The school can be public, private, or nonprofit as long as it is accredited. The money can be used to pay tuition and fees and buy books, supplies, and other

required equipment. Expenses for special-needs students also count. If the student is enrolled at least half-time, room and board also meet IRS expenses.

Q: My child has received a lot of savings bonds. How do these work?

A: Savings bonds come in low denominations, which has made them popular with smaller investors and as gifts for children's education funds. The interest income on EE bonds is exempt from state and local taxes. Federal taxes can be deferred until they are redeemed. Taxes also can be paid as they accrue, which is a tax-saving strategy for people who put the bonds in the children's names. Find out what interest rate you're earning on the bonds, though, because it may not be the highest-interest account.

Q: What is a UTMA/UGMA account?

A: The Uniform Gifts to Minors Act (UGMA) and Uniform Transfers to Minors Act (UTMA) are accounts that are set up as trust accounts for kids. The downside of these accounts is that when the child turns eighteen or twenty-one, depending on your state, he or she can access the money and can use it for whatever they want. They can go to school, buy a house – or blow it on a shiny red Corvette and take off into the sunset. These accounts also incur the "kiddie tax."

Q: What is the kiddie tax?

A: The kiddie tax is imposed on the UTMA and UGMA accounts. This is where the child pays taxes at the parent's tax bracket on the dollars. Taxes are paid every year on any dividend or interest income and could also be paid as capital gains when the money is used or an investment is sold.

Q: Is it possible to buy one share of stock from companies? I was considering buying stock as gifts for my grandchildren.

A: It's possible, but not the most effective or cost-efficient way to do it. You could buy the stock inside the Coverdell or UTMA/UGMA accounts but even then, buying just one share doesn't make a lot of sense financially. For example, say you buy this one share of stock for $90 and the stock goes up $5 per share, then you sell it. You actually lose money because it costs you money to buy and sell a stock; if it costs you $40 in commission to buy one share and $40 in commission to sell the share, then the stock price has to dramatically rise before you'd actually make any money. Stock is a great gift, but it would be better to save up some money for a while, then purchase a few shares so that it's worthwhile. Other considerations: If you used a Coverdell, you wouldn't have to worry about taxes as long as the money was used for higher education; there would be a tax issue, whether a gain or loss, if you buy the stock in an UTMA/UGMA account.

Q: My sister and brother-in-law are big spenders and their kids are growing up with the same lack of financial values. As their aunt I would like to give the kids some money for the holidays but don't want it spent on something that's a waste. What should I do?

A: You could open a Roth or Traditional IRA account in a child's name, if they have earned income. You can gift assets via a UGMA or UTMA custodial account, or in a trust account. You could fund a 529 plan or Coverdell account, or even gift shares of stock. Any of these options could be wonderful ways to introduce children to the benefits of long-term investing while giving you a break from holiday shopping stress. It also will give the child the gift of learning about investing, which is something that you cannot put a price tag on.

PROTECTING YOUR ASSETS

Most of us work so hard to gain assets such as a house, investments, or a business, yet so few of us take the time to put plans in place to protect them. Protecting your assets can mean a lot of things. If you have a business, it can mean making sure you have a succession plan so the business goes to whom you want. If you have assets and you pass away, it can mean having life insurance in place to replace lost income or to pay off liabilities for your dependents. Protecting assets can mean having enough liquid money to cover any emergency expenses. It can mean making sure you have health insurance, sheltering your assets from taxes or making sure your assets pass to the people you choose. Protecting your assets is doing estate planning such as setting up a health care directive, durable power of attorney, a will, or a trust. Protecting your assets doesn't just help you but your also helps your beneficiaries. My goal as a financial advisor is to help you save and accumulate enough money that you are your own insurance policy. The questions that follow give you some of the basics but be sure to seek out advice specific to your situation.

LIFE INSURANCE

Q: How do I know if I have the right coverage and the right types of insurance?
A: Too many people are talked into paying too much for life and disability insurance, whether by adding this coverage to loans, buying whole life insurance policies when term life insurance makes more sense, or buying life insurance when you have no dependents. However, you should have enough insurance to protect your dependents and your income in the case of death or disability. Review the insurance policies that you have and stay informed on the kind of policy you have, what you're paying for the policy, and when the policy is no longer in force before making decisions about purchasing more insurance; the trick is to have the right amount, but not pay too much for it.

Q: When should I buy life insurance?
A: You should purchase life insurance when you have liabilities to take care of or if you have someone who depends on your income. Let's say you're married and have two kids, both under the age of nine. You have a salary of $80,000 a year. Your spouse works part-time and takes care of the kids. If you died you would want to have a life insurance policy to pay off your liabilities, such as a mortgage or car loan, and to help your family keep their same standard of living, including in this case, for example, allowing your wife to continue to be able to stay at home with the kids.

Q: Is life insurance an investment?
A: No. Generally, you should buy life insurance and keep it separate from your investments. You buy insurance because you have a need: For example, if something happens to your spouse, you'd have the life insurance money to pay your debts, or if your spouse were to pass away, you'd have life insurance money to cover his or her monthly income.

Q: What is the difference between term and whole life insurance?

A: Two main types of life insurance are term and whole life. Term insurance is the least expensive type of insurance you can buy. It's for a set period, such as 10, 20, or 30 years. Say you buy a 20-year term insurance policy with a benefit of $500,000. If you pass away within those 20 years your beneficiaries would receive the $500,000. If you pass away after those 20 years are up, your beneficiaries wouldn't get any life insurance, but the goal is that by that time you will have accumulated enough assets to be your own insurance policy. Whole life insurance is for your whole life. It's more expensive, there is no set term and some of the money you spend in your premium goes into a cash value account. Most of the time you don't necessarily know how much you are paying for insurance and how much of your money is going to the cash value, which is basically a savings account.

Q: I have been looking at purchasing more life insurance on myself and have been looking into term insurance and whole life insurance. Which of these is the best?

A: It depends on your individual situation and what the insurance is for. Term insurance is the least expensive, but it is for a set period of time. If you just want insurance in place until you build up enough assets so you can afford to pay off all your liabilities, have enough to live on for the rest of your life, and provide your beneficiaries, then term insurance can be a good option.

Many financial advisors, including me, recommend term insurance for most people; it's less expensive and you can invest the difference you would have spent buying a whole life policy. It doesn't pay to have a cash value accruing in a whole life insurance policy if you cannot afford to max out your 401(k) and your IRAs.

Whole life insurance is more expensive, but it could be a good vehicle from an estate planning standpoint if you are looking to leave some money to your beneficiaries income-tax free or are looking to help with estate taxes.

Q: I think that I need to get an additional $250,000 term life insurance on my spouse now that we took on some more liabilities. What should I consider when looking at term life insurance?
A: There are a couple of things to keep in mind. First, make sure you find a good company that is credible and reliable. It's worth the money to choose a company that will be around in thirty years when you're going to need it. An independent insurance agent can help you compare companies and cost. As a general rule, on average it should cost you about $100 to $200 per year for every $100,000 worth of coverage depending on your health.

Q: Many years ago, I was "sold" a couple of whole life insurance policies. These have gradually built up cash value and I am trying to figure out if I should cash them in or keep paying into them. I also have a term policy as well as life insurance through my employer. Can you help me with this decision?
A: Yes. First, never get rid of an insurance policy before you have another in place just in case something were to happen. Cashing in insurance is not something you want to do lightly. Look at why you purchased it in the first place and if you still have a need for the insurance. You want to look at the cost of insurance as well as any tax implications. In a whole life policy you will have a taxable issue if you receive more money when you cash it in than you paid into the policy.

Q: We are having a baby and looking for additional life insurance coverage. Anyone will cover my husband but I had a stroke a few years back, and am having a hard time finding coverage. Any advice on how to find companies that will take a client with my history?

A: Talk to an independent insurance agent. An independent does not represent one particular company; he or she can help you compare costs and compare all the different insurance companies that have policies available to you with your situation. To find an independent insurance agent, ask your financial advisor.

HEALTH INSURANCE

Q: How do I know if I need disability insurance?

A: Disability insurance covers you as a worker in the event of an incident resulting in a disability. Disability insurance is there to replace your income if you are not able to perform your job; it's compensation for you as an injured worker for your loss of pay. Most employers provide some type of disability insurance plan for employees; however, it may not be enough and it may be short term, that is, it lasts only or less than 90 days. Talk to a financial advisor, who can help you evaluate the plan your employer provides and whether you need to buy more coverage.

Q: What are HSAs?

A: HSA stands for health savings account. These accounts are for you to save money for health care expenses. You can only have a health savings account if you have a high-deductible insurance plan. When you have an HSA, you pay a small amount every month as a premium on a health insurance plan. Then every month you also put money into a health savings account where you accumulate dollars. Then if something happens to you and you have a huge bill to pay you have money to cover your high deductible.

Q: What is COBRA insurance?

A: COBRA is health insurance that continues after you leave an employer if you don't have other health insurance coverage, such as coverage through a spouse's policy or through a new job. You can be on COBRA for eighteen months. COBRA insurance can also come into play in a divorce. If you are on your spouse's insurance plan and you get a divorce you cannot remain on your ex-spouse's health insurance. However, you can remain on COBRA for thirty-six months after a divorce. COBRA is good safety net to have, but it's expensive; you may be better off getting your own health insurance policy. When I resigned from my former broker dealer my COBRA quote was over $600 a month, which was outrageous. I was much better off purchasing my own health insurance policy. An individual health insurance policy could be less expensive because you have higher deductible and because you're not attached to a group where other high claims could have been processed in the past, driving up costs. Whichever option you choose, make sure you have some kind of coverage because health insurance is something that you cannot afford to live without.

Q: I have heard about LTC insurance. What is it and do I need it?

A: LTC stands for long-term care insurance. It's generally used to cover costs when you get older and need to pay for some kind of regular medical care, whether you continue to live in your own home or move to a nursing home. Most people start to decide whether they need long-term care insurance in their fifties or sixties, but many agents will tell you that LTC insurance can be purchased at any age. Talk to your financial advisor to see if this is something that fits for you.

Q: Who will make critical decisions about my health care if I am unable to do so?

A: The Terri Schiavo case brought the nation's attention to this difficult but important issue. The two most common forms of **advance directives**

are a living will and a durable power of attorney for health care, commonly referred to as a "health care proxy." A **living will** can explain in writing the care you wish to receive or avoid if you are incapacitated. A **health care proxy** allows you to legally designate someone to make medical decisions for you. Make sure you are prepared and have these two important documents in place. They will assure that you are getting the kind of care you want – or don't want – if you are unable to do so, based on decisions by the person(s) you choose. Doing so will also make it easier for your family and friends, because they'll know they're doing what you would want them to do.

Q: How do I designate a health care proxy?
A: Before you contact a lawyer about drafting an advance directive, you can save yourself time and trouble by understanding the types of issues the document should cover. Start by talking to your family and doctors about your medical wishes in as much detail as possible, outlining any information about the types of medical decisions that may come up based on your current health. Then have your attorney draw up your advance directive. You and several witnesses, usually two, will need to sign it. These witnesses cannot be related to you or be one of your beneficiaries. Once it is written, store it in a safe place with your other important documents and make sure your family and lawyer know where to find it. Also, give copies to anyone you have named as health care proxy, as well as to your doctor and a health care facility, such as a nursing home. Make sure you and/or your lawyer review this document at least once every five years. Get prepared and make sure you plan now for your future so you can save yourself some time and trouble.

DOCUMENTS TO PROTECT

Q: What is a POA?

A: POA stands for power of attorney. This is a legal document that allows someone to make decisions and act on your behalf. There is a power of attorney and **durable power of attorney**. The difference is a regular power of attorney ends if you are incapacitated, whereas a durable power of attorney does not. You want to have a durable power of attorney in place if you are out of town or in the event you're unable to sign documents such as checks, pay bills, or take care of your affairs. Anyone and everyone should have a durable power of attorney, even if you're married. For example, suppose your spouse goes into a coma and you want to take money out of his or her IRA or an account that's only in their name. You can only do so if there is written authorization – that is, durable power of attorney.

Q: What is durable power of attorney?

A: You can also designate a durable power of attorney for your financial affairs. As with a health care proxy, a durable power of attorney can specify how you want your financial affairs dealt with in case you become disabled or suffer a serious illness, and it designates someone who can make any financial decisions in your behalf. A big advantage of this "financial proxy" is that it can help prevent your loved ones from having to go to court to request guardianship over your financial affairs if you become incapacitated. This arrangement can also give the person the ability to pay your debts, manage investment transactions, and even make charitable gifts that could help reduce your estate taxes. So as you get your health care proxy in order, also remember to work on your financial proxy so you are also prepared for your finances.

Q: I have heard I should take inventory of the stuff in our home in case of a fire or disaster. Should I?

A: Yes. The Insurance Information Inst. has a website, www.knowyourstuff. org, where you can download home inventory software for free. A home inventory is a pictorial archive of all the "stuff" you own – not just your house, car, and computer but commonplace items such stereo systems and shoes. By doing this you can make sure you have enough insurance to cover your belongings, get insurance claims settled faster in the event of a loss, and substantiate losses for your income-tax returns.

Q: What documents do I need in place to protect myself?

A: At a minimum you want a durable power of attorney and a health care directive in place. Both are explained above. You also need a will or maybe even a trust in place to protect your assets that are not in a retirement account or life insurance policy.

Money Tip:

At a minimum, make sure you have a health care directive and a durable power of attorney.

ESTATE PLANNING

Q: What are some things I should consider when starting to think about our estate planning?

A: Did you do everything you need to do to communicate your wishes? There are a few things you want to make sure you've done. First, make certain you have a will. Also, be comfortable with the executors and trustee(s) you have selected. Second, don't forget to execute a living will or health care proxy in the event of catastrophic illness or disability. Third, having a living trust can help avoid probate. Lastly, if you have a living trust, have your assets titled in the name of the trust.

Q: I want to leave a legacy with my money. How do I do that?

A: First, congratulations on asking the question now so you can plan for your future. You have many options. Set up a plan with your financial advisor and an estate planning attorney. You may want to consider a trust or purchase a life insurance policy for a charity as a beneficiary.

Q: What questions should I ask to make sure I'm prepared my estate planning?

A: To start with:

- Have you updated your beneficiary designations on your existing life insurance policies?
- If you want to limit your spouse's flexibility regarding the inheritance, have you created a trust?
- Do you have the right amount and type of life insurance to pay your debts and to give your dependents enough money to replace your income and all estate settlement expenses?
- Have you considered creating trusts for family gift-giving?

These questions will help you figure out what you need to do in your estate planning to protect your family in the future.

Q: Why is it so important to have a will and where do I get one?

A: If you don't have a will, please go get one. Unfortunately, there are often two things that drive money: greed and fear. I have seen families torn apart because of money and lack of estate planning before a relative's death. See an attorney who specializes in estate planning to draw one up. You'll be glad you did, and more important, your family will thank you for protecting your assets.

Q: Why should I specifically hire an estate planning attorney? Can't I do my own will with a form I can download from the Internet?
A: If you do it yourself, you could end up doing it wrong. Even if you have help from a "lawyer friend" who doesn't specialize in estate planning, there could be problems with it, especially if someone decides to fight it. An attorney with specialized knowledge in estate planning and any special state or federal rules can do it correctly, and help reduce your anxiety and concerns. He or she knows how to help you minimize the amount of taxes on your estate, make sure your estate is kept intact when it is passed to your family, help you write your will, help you determine whether you want to set up a trust and if so, help you set it up.

Q: What is the difference between a will and a trust?
A: A will is a legal document that states where you want all your property (basically, all of your "stuff") to go. A trust is a legal document that states who you want to be in charge to make sure all your property gets to whomever you wanted it to go to. If you don't have a will or a trust then your estate will go into probate and a judge decides where your assets (and your stuff) goes. Obviously, you don't want someone else deciding for you, which is why, once again, it's so important to have a will and have it done professionally. It's also important to meet with an attorney who specializes in estate planning to make sure you have everything taken care of, especially because there are so many changes going on with estate planning and tax planning.

Q: When would I need a trust?
A: You want to meet with an estate planning attorney to help you determine this. Usually, if your estate net worth is over $2 million dollars, a trust could be written. You then can fund the trust account with your assets. A big mistake I see people make is setting up a trust but not actu-

ally funding it. You want to work closely with your attorney and with your financial advisor to help protect your assets.

Q: When should I update my will?

A: You should update your will any time there is a life change – for example, a divorce, a death, birth of a child, marriage, or even if you change your mind about who you want your property to go to. You also should update it if laws change relating to estate planning and your situation. A will can be updated easily with an estate planning attorney. And remember just to review your will and other estate planning documents periodically, even if no life change has taken place.

Q: In the years ahead I will transfer a large amount of my wealth to my heirs, but I don't want them to have to pay more than their fair share of estate tax. How can I be sure my estate passes to the next generation in the most tax-efficient manner possible?

A: You want to look at all your assets, how they are titled and what kinds of accounts you have. For example, life insurance generally passes tax-free to your named beneficiaries whereas money in a Traditional IRA does not. Roth IRA assets pass to your beneficiaries without taxes whereas your 401(k) doesn't. Traditional IRAs and 401(k)'s will have income taxes on withdrawal. There also could be a tax on your whole estate. It may not be in your best interest to have most of your money in retirement accounts (such as IRAs or 401(k)s) because these assets will pass to your beneficiaries and they will have to pay income taxes on these dollars. With the exception of the Roth IRA, that vehicle is income tax-free on qualified withdrawals. There are a number of other ways to pass on money and assets to your heirs. You want an estate plan that can help you accomplish your financial objectives such as funding higher education for future generations and providing for loved ones' futures. So, for example, did you know that now, in any given year anyone can gift up to $12,000 a year without triggering the gift tax? That means neither you nor the recipient pays taxes. And with the 529 plan you can speed up gifting for five years. This means that today you could take $60,000 from Grandma and $60,000 from Grandpa and all of a sudden you have the money out of Grandma and Grandpa's estate, plus little Johnny has $120,000 in his 529 plan to help him with college education; however, you will not be able to make additional contributions for five years. You could also set up trust accounts to place assets in trust.

Q: My husband of fifty years passed away, leaving me and our eight kids with wonderful memories, and also his life insurance. How should I distribute the money among my kids when a few of them have a greater need for financial support than others? Do you know of any policies or strategies in this area? And where do you recommend I put my extra money?

A: I would definitely sit down with your financial advisor and an estate planning attorney. You know your kids better than anyone else does, so it's really up to you whether to give more to some than to others. What I can tell is that you need to develop a plan, and you may want to look at gifting money. Currently, anyone can gift up to $12,000 a year per person without you having to pay taxes. I helped one of my clients set up trust accounts for his kids (who were all over the age of fifty). Dad has since passed away, but each received a portion of his estate; some of the kids received $500 a month and the others received $1,000 a month. Because of the way the trust was set up, this is a gift they'll have for their lifetime. You may also want to look at adding to your IRAs or consider setting up a trust account for the rest of the assets.

Q: I left the beneficiary designation blank when I opened my retirement accounts. Is this OK?

A: Generally, I don't let clients do this. You want to name someone who will receive the assets if something were to happen to you. Otherwise, where your assets go will depend on the custodial agreement or plan document that governs your retirement plan assets; this may or may not be what you had intended.

Q: What if I put my beneficiary for my IRA account as my estate?

A: You don't want to do this – if you do, the IRA assets could end up in probate court, along with the rest of your estate. Instead, specifically list each individual you want to receive your IRA assets at your death. Talk to your financial advisor to make sure your beneficiary designation forms are filled out correctly. You want to be aware and understand what your beneficiary designations are so you are prepared, so make sure that all your beneficiaries are correct.

Q: My father has some land that he would like to transfer to me. Is there a way to do this without taxes?

A: I can't say it often enough: Sit down with an estate planning attorney. There are a number of trusts you can set up which may be an option for you. Of course it always depends on your overall situation, but the one thing you want to be aware of is when you receive assets after someone's death, you get a step up in "basis," whereas if you receive the land as a gift from your father while he is still alive, you "inherit" his basis. This means that if you receive the land from your father after he passed away your cost basis is what the land is worth the day your father died, not what your father's basis was. This comes into play particularly if you want to sell the land. Let's say your father bought his home in 1980 for $100,000 and on the date of his death it's worth $500,000. If you receive the asset after his death and sell it for $500,000, you wouldn't have to pay any capital gains taxes. On the other hand, if your father gave you the house as a gift while he is still alive, and you sold the house for $500,000 – even after his death – you would have a capital gain of $400,000 since his – now your – basis would be $100,000.

Q: I can gift money to as many people as I want without paying taxes on it, right?

A: Yes, you can gift up to $12,000 per year to as many people as you want without triggering the gift tax.

Q: I just inherited some money and am clueless about what to do. Can you direct me to some help?

A: You need a financial advisor to help you wade through all your options and help you develop a plan that fits you. It is so smart of you to ask for some financial help because so many people who receive a chunk of money find they just blow it all. It is so important to use windfalls like these to help you achieve your goals and dreams. A financial advisor can walk you through all your options, all the different types of accounts that are available to you, and help you develop a plan that fits you.

Q: When I contribute to different charities should I donate cash?

A: Consider donating stock instead of cash, especially if your stocks are highly appreciated. Not only will you still help the charity, you will avoid taxes on any gains on the stock. (The charity does not have to worry about taxes on stock.) You can also deduct the full value of the shares on your tax return for the year, so it's a win-win for everyone. It works like this: Say you sell $3,000 worth of stock and had to pay $800 in capital gains taxes, then donated the money to the charity; the charity would only have $2,200 and you would have to pay the $800 in tax. On the other hand, if you donated $3,000 worth of stock and the charity sold it, the charity would get the full $3,000. So you're not only helping the charity, you're helping yourself on your next tax return. I'm sure the charity will be happy to help you with the paperwork for your donation.

Q: Is naming a charity as one of multiple beneficiaries a good idea?

A: Not always. This is an excellent time to create a separate IRA for the amount to be paid to the charity upon your death. The charity, unlike your heirs, can receive the IRA benefit free of estate and income tax. Because of special tax breaks for charities, the IRA assets will be worth more to the charity than the after-tax amount that would be available to your heirs.

Q: What is probate tax and how does it affect me and my estate?

A: Probate is the legal process of settling your estate in court. An estate goes into probate when there is no will or if the will is contested; this is why you want to do some estate planning. Probate laws apply to the estates of people who were residents of the state they lived in at the time of their death. Probate also applies to other states' residents who own real estate, such as a house, building, and/or land, in another state. Some kinds of property and assets don't need to be probated. These include property owned as joint tenants, jointly held bank accounts, payable-on-death accounts, transfer-on-death accounts, life insurance proceeds to a specific beneficiary, and retirement benefits with a designated beneficiary in the event you die.

Q: I want to give money to my grandkids for college as a lump sum, but if I do this don't I have to worry about gift taxes?

A: You can gift up to $12,000 per year per person without triggering the gift tax, and with the 529 plan you can speed that up for five years. So if you wanted to give a lump sum to your grandkids for college, you could gift up to $60,000 per grandchild today as an individual, up to $120,000 today as a married couple. However, you'll then have to wait another five years to gift $12,000 a year. Withdrawals for the child if used for qualified educational expenses are tax-free. Withdrawals not used for higher education are subject to taxes.

Q: I have heard of a Stretch IRA. What exactly is this and how does it work?

A: I don't know how many people you know who inherit money and just blow it all within a few months (or sometimes even a few days)? There's something called a Stretch IRA that allows you to control how your beneficiaries receive money after your death. I believe this is one of the best gifts that you can give. It's much better for someone to receive $1,000 a month for the rest of their life than a few hundred thousand dollars to foolishly spend, with nothing to show for it. And with no planning, your heirs could incur many unnecessary income and estate tax issues. Although there are limitations, with proper planning an IRA could provide a lifetime of income for the owner or the beneficiaries.

Q: My sister passed away and I have her Traditional IRA now. What should I do with this account?

A: You want to take this account and make it a beneficiary IRA. This will give you more control. You can then take this money out within five years or based on your life expectancy. You can also take the money out but you will be paying state and federal income taxes.

Q: I just received a large inheritance and never had a big chunk of money land in my lap like this. What do I do with this money?

A: It's important to let that money sit in an account until you are emotionally and financially ready to deal with this. If it were a bitter divorce or your spouse died suddenly in a difficult death, you should leave that money in a money market account for at least a few weeks or months until you feel comfortable and completely understand what you are doing with this money. Take all the time that you need.